AFTER THE WAR:
ESSAYS ON RECENT SPANISH POETRY

SALVADOR JIMÉNEZ-FAJARDO
AND
JOHN C. WILCOX, *EDITORS*

AFTER THE WAR: ESSAYS ON RECENT SPANISH POETRY

SOCIETY OF SPANISH AND SPANISH-AMERICAN STUDIES

The Society of Spanish and Spanish-American Studies promotes bibliographical, critical and pedagogical research in Spanish and Spanish-American studies by publishing works of particular merit in these areas. On occasion, the Society also publishes creative works. SSSAS is a non-profit educational organization sponsored by the University of Colorado at Boulder. It is located in the Department of Spanish and Portuguese, University of Colorado, Campus Box 278, Boulder, Colorado 80309-0278, U.S.A.

International Standard Book Number (ISBN): 0-89295-055-2

Library of Congress Catalog Card Number: 88-61768

Printed in the United States of America

Impreso en los Estados Unidos de América

This text was prepared on the Xerox Star word processing system by Sandy Adler, Foreign Language Word Processing Specialist for the College of Arts and Sciences, University of Colorado at Boulder.

CONTENTS

PREFACE

The present collection offers a selection of the papers presented at the 1984 Illinois Wesleyan University's Fifth Colloquium on Literature: Spanish Poetry Since 1939. The Colloquium brought together scholars from around the country to discuss both established and recent trends in a genre whose resurgence has acquired remarkable momentum since the sixties. The extraordinary energy of contemporary Spanish poetry, however, does not diminish the importance of that written during the forties and fifties, for the genre was graced, even in the bleakest post-Civil War years, by the presence of strong individual talents who maintained unbroken the exceptional quality of Peninsular poetry in this century.

John Wilcox is right in evoking Ricardo Gullón's term *generación escindida* when he speaks of the first postwar group of poets and in questioning the usefulness of the generational label, which Spanish criticism uses with insistence and seemingly against all evidence. It seems idle to insist on such labels when they have no relational function unless one seeks levels of generality whose referential significance fades into abstraction. It may be possible, however, in a much less binding sense, to mention certain *tendencias de grupo*, keeping in mind that the panorama of postwar poetry is as much one of individual talents as it is one of movements.

John Wilcox, in the admirably informed historical survey with which this collection opens, makes passing reference to the ideological differences that left their mark on post-Civil War poetry. These differences were to be transformed into theoretical distinctions involving attention to or avoidance of reality, since the political climate allowed for no clear expression of ideology unless it approved of the régime. And yet, such ideology is implicit in the two groups that defined themselves within the post-war climate: the *garcilasistas* with their traditional thrust toward the evidence of form, and the poets of *Espadaña*, whose attention to dreary reality was reflected in anguished fragmentation.

Such are the historical roots of that curious phenomenon in Spanish poetry of the past decades: the incessant effort at redefinition that critics and anthologizers engage in. Anthologies seek to establish 'the' canon every few years, to trace antecedents and evoke tendencies, while strong voices (Otero, Hierro, Celaya, González, Rodríguez, Brines) assert themselves independently. It is not with movements that contemporary poetry links itself, but with individuals such as Antonio Machado, Juan Ramón Jiménez, Luis Cernuda, Vicente Aleixandre, Miguel Hernández, Jorge Guillén. Strong poets have recognized that the initial opposition between formalism and

7

realism was superficial. They have sought intrinsic elements of lyricism that both precede and supersede such facile distinctions.

The essays that follow John Wilcox's survey attend precisely to such elements as they characterize Peninsular poetry of the past fifty years. Our panorama of critical views begins with Andrew Debicki's masterful keynote talk and concludes most appropriately with Biruté Ciplijauskaité's considerations of the renovated importance of the poetic *word* and the recognition of Guillén's continued significance in the work of several key young poets. All the essays linking Debicki's historical redefinitions to Ciplijauskaité's focused analysis address issues of poetic practice and theoretical relevance. These issues intersect with the principal poetic trends in Europe and America and reflect the major importance of Peninsular poetry in our century.

In his "Three Moments of Post-Civil War Spanish Poetry," Andrew Debicki dismisses from the outset, as possessing insufficient explanatory power, the early distinction between formalist and realist poetry. He prefers to focus on the way succeeding groups of poets have exploited language. He identifies as a sustained trend of increasing importance the means whereby poetry variously includes its own reading as a constitutive element of its composition. As early as in Dámaso Alonso's *Hijos de la ira* (1944), Debicki points out, the mixture of several levels of expression involved the reader in the production of its significance and of its configuration. Already in Alonso's collection we notice a departure from the symbolist tradition of a poem's self-sufficient and necessarily cohesive form. To achieve the efficacy of open form (though somewhat later), Blas de Otero will make extensive use of intertextual and collage techniques, while Gabriel Celaya will rely principally on striking juxtapositions of the abstract and the concrete which Debicki labels "systems breakage." These are all means of breaching the poem's formal isolation from the vital context, emphasizing the situational component of poetry.

In Debicki's classic description, the poets for whom Alonso, Otero and Celaya were already elders see in poetry an "act of discovery." Meaning arises from a process in which the reader is insistently solicited as co-participant in an esthetic evaluation of human experience. This poetry begins the great challenge to its own and the reader's expectations of esthetic vision which is pursued still in the areas of concrete and conceptual poetry. The reader's share in the process has grown, as has the realm of experience that is investigated and now includes: the boundaries between naturalness and artistry (Claudio Rodríguez); the challenging of customary codes for organizing reality (Angel González); the utility of language as a means of investigating previously unrecognized layers of experience (José Angel Valente). The entire realm of linguistic expression has become an instrument for understanding because it is the principal, some would say the only, constituent of our epistemology.

Not so for the poets whom Debicki identifies as representing the third and latest moment in Peninsular poetry. These young poets are skeptical about the ability of language to "discover" reality and about the poet's capacity, indeed his responsibility, to assume, even implicitly, such inclusive duties. They are more interested in underlining the aleatory status of the poetic task, giving renewed importance to esthetic concerns. Theirs is, however, an assertive esthetic stance, in which language is not so much asked to investigate reality, but to create it. Reality is what words can construct in the tripartite cooperation between poet, poem and reader. The ludic element of linguistic invention gains ground. The poem is an open-ended system through which circulate freely the traces of other esthetic codes. It may assert a distanced viewpoint that serves to frame the intense vividness of life, or it may create a portion of reality as it questions its own means of creation. In each instance it seeks to renew the reader's transaction with language and with art. Not surprisingly, poets such as Guillermo Carnero, Amparo Amorós and Pere Gimferrer find aspects of their practice in the work of such predecessors as Cernuda, Aleixandre, or the Surrealists, but also in that of Guillén and even in Modernism. It should not in the least surprise us that these young poets choose to forge new links with their past. But they look back upon the work of earlier figures with a postmodern sensibility. This sensibility disregards past conceptions of internal form and attaches itself to the intuitions of dislocating perspectivism in Cernuda, to the isolation of the aleatory esthetic moment in Guillén, or it endorses the attack on customary referentiality characteristic of Surrealism.

As Andrew Debicki points out, his retrospective does not pretend to encompass all of the poetry written since 1939, though it does treat the principal trends. Two related characteristics of this poetry stand out: the notion of the poetic text as 1. the locus of circulating levels and modes and language and 2. the locus of a co-creative interaction between poet and reader. Such open texts anticipate ever-renewed readings which forge vital connections with each reader and the context of his attention.

There is a ludic element in the manipulation of the poetic word and in the esthetic tradition that characterizes postmodernism which becomes increasingly noticeable in the latest poetry. No longer, we may venture to say, does poetry 'mean' in the way in which we usually understand the word. It does not invite a single hypostasized notion, nor is it an object that 'is,' as New Critics were fond of saying. The implication of such attitudes was that artistic objects bore their own implicit, self-sufficient significance. Now, one's reading enters into play, responds to the solicitation of a language game which is not, however, an intranscendent exercise. The ludic pleasures of linguistic invention have never been absent from the poetic craft. Poems are penetrated by intertexts and assume more often a colloquial tone. These are qualities that typify much of the best poetry of the sixties and seventies. It is a poetry that frequently renews and transforms our attention to earlier texts. It shows a marked tendency to open-endedness and seeks to renew its language by rejecting stylistic and lexical boundaries. Maria Stycos's "Intertextuality in Selected Spanish Poets Since 1939: Intertext/Poetics/Reader," explores the practice of intertextual play in the work of Angel González, Francisco Brines and Gloria Fuertes. González is especially interested in drawing upon the reader's memory of other texts — Bécquer and Jiménez are the selected instances — thereby instituting a creative tension between his contribution and the reader's own: poet and reader function as both reader and poet. González, though down to earth and untrammeled in his expression, regenerates through the tension binding the text to the participants the aura of mystery, the magic overtones that distinguish the poetic word. The focus on intertextual tensions also allows Stycos a point of entry into the difficult poetry of Francisco Brines, whose contrastive use of Juan Ramón Jiménez's images serves to highlight his own despair when he confronts what he considers the impreciseness and flimsiness of words. Should the rift between the poet and his language widen, only silence can emerge. As for Gloria Fuertes, she also uses Juan Ramón Jiménez to affirm, in contrast, her own preference for concrete, if impure, existence. It is the sensual presence of the body that interests her, not its symbolism.

The confidence of Juan Ramón Jiménez, who asked: "Intelijencia, dame el nombre exacto de las cosas," is no longer available to the poets of recent decades. But this does not mean that they reject the power of the poetic word, only that they put it to different uses, less exalted perhaps, but not necessarily less powerful. In "Posturas del poeta ante su palabra en la España de la posguerra," Douglass Rogers addresses the poet's evolving view of the poetic word as both instrument and topic of poetry. By attending to the poets' comments on their own work as well as to their creative texts, he finds that the polarization of the estheticist and realistic trends in postwar poetry is a superficial phenomenon. He suggests that a radical change of orientation took place in the sixties, involving not so much that dichotomy but the poets' fundamental understanding of the 'word.'

Rogers traces a metapoetic vein in Peninsular poetry back to the symbolist tradition represented by such poets as Jiménez (word as incantation), Salinas (mythifying power of words) and Guillén (naming as being). Vicente Aleixandre had himself begun to turn away from this path before the War, but it was in the so-called "realist" school of *Espadaña* that the reaction became clearest. During the first two decades following the Civil War, poets expected poetic language to communicate the 'real.' But, while they formally rejected anything that might hint at an exalted connotation in poetic language, at an underlying level the mystery of words could still compel them. José Hierro, for instance, a 'naming' poet, will express a love for "marvellous words" that is not too remote from that of the Antonio Machado "soñador." These poets, Rogers suggests, while trying to discard past rhetoricism, cannot avoid a rhetoric of their own.

Perhaps as a result of Saussurian structuralism, a new linguistic awareness becomes noticeable on the intellectual horizon of the sixties. Poets such as José María Valverde and Angel González, though they prefer ordinary language, display increasing linguistic sophistication. González will focus on the materiality of the poem, while maintaining at the same time an ironic distance from the concept of 'exalted' creation. In his view, the work of the poet may be described, for instance, as the search for some single concrete word within a poem. Together with a preference for the open-ended text that seeks the reader's participation, the individual poetic function is drastically reduced in scope. Nevertheless, the notion persists of the "true word" (Valente). Likewise, one still encounters the recognition of poetic creation as a creation of words whose underlying affinities remain, to a degree, unplumbed. These poets pay close attention to the idea of the 'poetic,' making it often the very subject of their texts. The *word* may have been brought down to earth from its pedestal, but its creative force remains uncontested.

As we have noted, the work of Angel González reflects the most important trends in Peninsular poetry since the sixties. María Stycos observed his use of intertexts, and Douglass Rogers examined his interpretation of the concept of a 'poetic word.' There is general agreement among critics and readers that González's is a major poetic voice in post-war Spain. The two papers that follow approach his work from different though related angles. In *"Différance* in the Early Poetry of Angel González," Margaret Persin investigates the stylistic strategies that the poet uses to transform the reader into a co-creator of the poem; Martha Miller, in "The Ludic Poetry of Angel González," examines in particular the poet's practice of 'metapoetry' and his manipulation of 'nonsense' to generate several levels of meaning.

Margaret Persin describes the experimental tactics employed by González to generate his reader's responses. González's openended texts require the reader's mediation to achieve temporary fulfillment. The absence, or gap, that elicits our supplementation may be generated by dialectical developments to whose antithesis we must supply a thesis and a synthesis, by syntactical structures that call for completion, or by lexical indeterminacies that we may seek to fixate. Such devices are intended to implicate the reader in an overall dialectical interchange between absence and presence. The poetic text then appears as the starting point of creation rather than its actual manifestation.

González achieves similar effects through his use of intertextual reference, nonsense games and metapoetry. Martha Miller finds that metapoetry makes its appearance in the earliest of the poet's texts and assumes an important role in the seventies. By analyzing the frames generated in a recent González poem, Martha Miller isolates the devices that actively undermine the notion of unitary meaning. Principally, these devices are semantic crossovers and the clash of logical categories. The result is a ludic text ever available to renewal.

The response that the poetry of Francisco Brines seeks from his readers is frequently in the nature of an existential meditation. Judith Nantell, in "Writing and Reading: Dialectical Correlations in Francisco Brines's *Insistencias en Luzbel*," comments on the poet's exploration of authentic and inauthentic modes of being and his notion of the poem's origin as an ontological phenomenon, realized as modes of writing. She addresses as well the corresponding modes of reading that such poetry requires. Nantell shows how Brines's poems can be both investigative tools and devices of survival, for the writer and for the reader. The reader completes the poem as he collaborates in its enactment, and as he deciphers the text, the reader deciphers a projection of his own self. At the same time the poet/speaker secures a portion of immortality through the future readers who recreate both his and their own presence, inexhaustibly, in the poem. For Brines the poet's existence, his poetry, is fulfilled by others, but through it those others are led to questions involving the reciprocity of writing and reading, of creating and being.

It is not the ontological but the ludic component of poetry that has attracted younger poets since the seventies. Not that there should be a divorce between these two aspects of poetry. One may best be able to project the fundamental concerns of the art by accentuating its aleatory nature. The Baroque poets understood this very well. Today various arts, and conceptual art in general, focus precisely on the very constituents of creation. Ignacio-Javier López, in "Poesía 'conceptual' en España: La producción de Ignacio Prat," assesses the possible communicative exchanges that the reader may attempt with the experimental work of this difficult critic-poet. López endeavors to show that even though Prat seemed to address his poetry to a limited number of friends and 'initiates,' there is much more to it than games of difficulty.

Prat's poetry is about art itself, about poetry itself. At this juncture that is nothing new. But his work attempts to incorporate as well the role of the critic, or mediator, by elaborating within itself the space of reflection. Under these conditions López ventures *not* to interpret, but merely to describe and present the poet's work. He shows that Prat's reflection on the nature of poetry, which already takes as its origin a double gloss (Pere Gimferrer, a prominent member of Castellet's *Nueve Novísimos* 1970 anthology, rewriting Jiménez), though it may appear as mere virtuosity, becomes a means of signaling both the merit and the aleatoriness of the artistic gesture. The reader is drawn to the game of language and contributes his own creativity, not as a mediator but as a new inventor.

It is perhaps in instances of striking experimentalism that we discover the most fundamental continuities. The language games of Ignacio Prat revitalize in us the sense of wonder and fun, the exhilaration before the endless possibilities of words that poets have expressed across the ages. But there is also another vein in recent poetry, one in which linguistic self-reference is joined to a persistent awareness of composition and the need to renovate the transcendence of words. In her featured address, Biruté Ciplijauskaité, as an homage to the recently deceased Jorge Guillén, examines his impact on the work of several younger poets. While Guillén's voice seems not as evident in recent Spanish poetry as that of, for instance, Aleixandre, or Cernuda, Biruté Ciplijauskaité discerns, during the seventies, renewed interest in some of the most prominent features of his work. She notes an intensified attention to the intrinsic worth of words, the merging of the ethical and the esthetic, a vigorous confrontation of reality, the idea of the 'finished' poem.

Ciplijauskaité does not imply that every one of these traits is identifiable within each of the poets that she presents. In María Victoria Atencia she underlines an affirmative stance before reality which translates into the effort to capture joyful instants by means of exact words. Alejandro Amusco uses compact oriental forms — the tanka for instance — to elicit the essential power of language. His careful placing of words in near-necessary patterns generates a singular "irradiating" force that seems to draw upon the very essence of poetry. Luis Suñén also prefers shorter pieces. His is an organized enthusiasm, a rigorous, precise enunciation of substantives. As in Guillén, one finds in this poet the emotion of form that unites technical mastery to a passionate encounter with materiality. Jaime Siles is likewise intent on uncovering the basic substance of nouns. He conceives the task of the poet as the return to reality but is assailed by a fundamental skepticism that ultimately leads him towards the unsay-

13

able and to silence. While this seems to run counter to the thrust of Guillén's poetry, Siles retains from his elder an emphasis on form, the art of the counterpoint and the sense of the poem as constructed language. With an impressive condensation of means, Siles's poetry appears to move inexorably towards night and emptiness.

All four poets, to varying degrees, display noticeable affinities with Guillén. They have kept his emphasis on form and on its intrinsic 'value.' For them also, the poet's craft appears as an ethical responsibility, a personally necessary task. The presence of Jorge Guillén has acted selectively on a limited number of poets, but his attitude, Biruté Ciplijauskaité feels, is as an interior light in their poetry.

It was away from any *tendencias de grupo* that these poets defined their work, intent on personal readings of a tradition of individuals, with Guillén figuring prominently in this tradition. We return in this final essay to evaluations implicit in the first one (Debicki) and that were confirmed in various ways through all the essays in between. Paradoxically, during a period rich in anthologies, in the definition of new movements, the birth and demise of many review-centered groups of poets, and the proliferation of 'regionalisms,' the poets whose impact is most profound are those who supersede all such grouping. There *are* recognizable tendencies: the growing importance of the reader's participation, the legitimation of all levels of language, the pervasive appearance of irony and skepticism, the undermining of traditional poetic closure. They signal changing attitudes toward the artistic process in general which are distinctive, perhaps, of our postmodern world. And yet, these tendencies do not conspicuously affect the poetry of some of the most promising younger poets. As this collection of essays demonstrates, the continuing vitality of the genre in Spain, though it accommodates trends and schools as well, is warranted by individuals whose singular talent stands out indifferent to fashions.

Salvador Jiménez-Fajardo
Illinois Wesleyan University

SPANISH POETRY
FROM THE MID 1930s TO THE MID 1980s:
AN INTRODUCTION

John Wilcox
University of Illinois-Urbana

Toward the beginning of the third decade of the twentieth century, poetic sensibility in the Spanish Peninsula underwent a change. Optimism, which in certain respects characterized the 1920s — "¡Oh luna, cuánto abril, / Qué vasto y dulce el aire! / Todo lo que perdí / Volverá con las aves" — gradually yielded to anger and anguish. In 1929, Rafael Alberti (b. 1902) published *Sobre los ángeles*, and Federico García Lorca (1898-1936) began *Poeta en Nueva York* (publ. 1940). The surrealistic style of these two books of poetry, coupled with their sense of alienation, are also found in the work of Luis Cernuda (1902-1963), who between 1932 and 1933 was at work on *Donde habite el olvido*. A few haunting lines from that book — "Soy eco de algo" (III), "No es el amor quien muere, / Somos nosotros mismos" (XII) — can epitomize the anguished sentiment of the early 1930s; they can also hint at what is called the *neo-romantic* strain to 1930s' poetry in Spain. An additional characteristic of this poetry, described as "humane," is a desire to give voice to the suffering and compassion of people of flesh and bone. This *rehumanized* poetic — "una poesía impura como un traje" — clearly manifested itself in 1935, in the first issue of Pablo Neruda's journal *Caballo verde para la poesía*.

There is an intricate pattern to the ebb and flow of new waves in Spanish poetry since the mid 1930s, but the humane, the neo-romantic, and the surreal are, quite often, a part of the tide.

This introduction can only indicate the first appearance of new poets and poetics in five successive movements in Spanish poetry since the 1930s [1]

I. Mid 1930s to Mid 1940s

The first new voice in Spanish poetry — after the glorious "Silver Age" of the 1920s — is considered to be that of Luis Rosales (b. 1910), who in *Abril* (1935) juxtaposed his awe and love for nature — "¡oh maravilla sin huella!" — with a deep reverence for its Creator. The combination — love for land, family, God — becomes a hallmark of the period.

Rosales forms part of a motley group of poets which literary historians cannot agree on calling the "Generation of 36." In addition to Rosales, the poets associated with this disputed generation are: Luis Felipe Vivanco (1907-1975); the brothers Juan Panero (1908-1937) and Leopoldo Panero (1909-1962); Miguel Hernández (1910-1942); José Luis Cano (b. 1912); Ildefonso Manuel Gil (b. 1912); Dionisio Ridruejo (1912-1975); José García Nieto (b. 1914); Germán Bleiberg (b. 1915); José María Valverde (b. 1926).[2]

In terms of political ideology, these poets were certainly "split" — "escindida" being Ricardo Gullón's term for this generation. Some were Republicans (Hernández, Bleiberg) and others Nationalists (Ridruejo), but their work in general evinces a religious feeling toward man and God, focuses on the landscape of Spain, and meditates on love and death; in all such respects, their work is — in Dámaso Alonso's term — arraigada ("rooted poetry"). In addition, in as much as this body of work evades the reality of the Spanish Civil War, foregrounds melody, and reveals a marked preference for the matter and manner of Renaissance verse (in particular the sonnet), it shares a common interest and style.

These poets are known as garcilasistas, after Garcilaso de la Vega (1501-1536), the fourth centenary of whose death was celebrated in 1936.[3] Bleiberg's Sonetos amorosos (1936) can epitomize the "garcilasista" style: "El alma te construye entre azucenas / sobre el paisaje que la brisa hiere, / donde los aires tiemblan en tu ensueño." As a group, they had their own journals: Escorial, founded in 1940, edited by Ridruejo and supported by the Falange; and Garcilaso, founded in 1943 and edited by José García Nieto.

Of the above poets, the work of Luis Rosales is today undergoing serious re-evaluation, especially the impact of his subsequently influential La casa encendida. The poetry of Miguel Hernández, which spans three generations, from the 1920s to the 1940s, has already left its indelible mark. Initially, it is baroque (Perito en lunas [1933]), then replete with existential anguish (El rayo que no cesa [1936]), and finally it expresses a social, even revolutionary fervor (Viento del pueblo [1937], El hombre acecha [1939]).[4] Hernández is one of the principal models for the next group of Spanish poets.

II. Mid 1940s to Mid 1950s

The precursors of the next group of poets — Miguel de Unamuno and Antonio Machado — died at the end of the 1930s (1937 and 1939 respectively). In the mid-1940s Spanish poetry ceased to be as genteel as it had been heretofore. Poets began to deal in their work with the horror of everyday existence in a bitterly divided post-Civil War society; they began to give expression to the grief, disgruntlement, and gall that had been festering in their hearts. These changed attitudes were foregrounded in 1944, the year in which the journal Espadaña was founded, and in which Dámaso Alonso and Vicente Aleixandre began publishing a different type of poetry, different, that is, both for them and from previous Spanish poetry. This changed

16

vision is subsequently manifested in the work of a group of poets who began writing in the late 1940s and who became known through anthologies published in the early 1950s. José Luis Cano christened them "la primera generación poética de posguerra."[5] *Espadaña*, founded in León in 1944 by Eugenio de Nora, Victoriano Crémer, and Father Antonio G. de Lama (who quickly resigned), set itself up in opposition to the *garcilasista* attitude to reality. It insisted that poetry be committed — following Machado — to the moment in time in which the poet lived, that it concern itself with man and surrounding reality. In short, it believed that poetry had to be socially committed (*engagé*, "comprometida"). In *Espadaña* there is a *rehumanizing* zeal, and it stands in stark contrast to the *dehumanizing* tendencies of the two previous movements in Spanish poetry: the Generations of 27 and 36.

Dámaso Alonso, however, will stand as the prototypical *rehumanizer* of the period with two shatteringly original books of poetry, both published in 1944, *Oscura noticia* and *Hijos de la ira*. Alonso's poetry is *arraigada*, because it is frequently an apostrophe to God; however, it is *desarraigada* ("unrooted") because, for the poetic persona, faith is not a facile given but an anguished struggle. Also, Alonso's poems describe human existence in all its misery. In addition, his verse, which avoids all the traditional prosodic forms of Spanish poetry, is — in its diction — colloquial, even prosaic. The following lines form the core of "Insomnio":

Y paso largas horas preguntándole a Dios, preguntándole
    por qué se pudre lentamente mi alma,
por qué se pudren más de un millón de cadáveres en esta
    ciudad de Madrid,
por qué mil millones de cadáveres se pudren lentamente en
    el mundo

But as another poem from *Hijos de la ira* makes clear, Alonso's is a struggle toward God, not a rejection of him; "De Profundis" presents the speaker in all his unworthiness:

Pero desde la mina de las maldades, desde el pozo de la
    miseria,
mi corazón se ha levantado hasta mi Dios,
y le ha dicho: Oh Señor, tú que has hecho también la
    pobredumbre,
mírame,
yo soy el orujo exprimido en el año de la mala cosecha,
yo soy el excremento del can sarnoso,
el zapato sin suela en el carnero del camposanto,
yo soy el montoncito de estiércol a medio hacer, que nadie
    compra,

y donde casi ni escarban las gallinas.
Pero te amo,
pero te amo frenéticamente.

This *tremendista* ("extreme") poetry parallels the *tremendismo* in the novels of that time, especially Camilo José Cela's *La familia de Pascual Duarte*, which also appeared in 1944. It is a squeal — rather than a cry — from the depths of a tyrannized heart.

In Alonso's verse, protest is implicit, but poetry of social protest was developed in the work of poets who gained recognition in a number of anthologies that began appearing in the early 1950s. The poetry of this group is undoubtedly rooted in life, but is considered "desarraigada" as it is not "rooted" in the traditional religious values of Catholic Spain. God and religion, for those poets of the fifties for whom they were a concern, are an anguished, existential struggle (as indeed they were for Unamuno). The most salient characteristics of this group are commitment to everyday reality, a concern to speak to an *immense majority* of people (about life, love, death), and a preference for non-traditional stanzas and meters.

Poets associated with this new wave in Spanish poetry include: Angela Figuera (1902-84), Carmen Conde (b. 1907), Victoriano Crémer (b. 1908), Gabriel Celaya (b. 1911), Ramón de Garciasol (b. 1913), Blas de Otero (1961-79), Gloria Fuertes (b. 1918), Leopoldo de Luis (b. 1918), Vicente Gaos (1919-80), José Luis Hidalgo (1919-47), Rafael Morales (b. 1919), José Hierro (b. 1922), Carlos Bousoño (b. 1923), and Eugenio de Nora (b. 1923).[6] The clearest examples of what is thought of as social poetry for this time can be found in the work of Hierro, Celaya, Otero, and Figuera.[7]

The poetry of José Hierro contains both deep personal anguish and implicit social protest. In *Quinta del 42* (1952), there is an apostrophe to Spain, "Canto a España," in which the poetic voice exclaims:

Oh España, qué vieja y qué seca te veo.
. . .
Qué tristes he visto a tus hombres.
. . .
Les pides que pongan sus almas de fiesta.
No sabes que visten de duelo, que llevan a cuestas el peso
    de tu acabamiento,
que ven impasibles llegar a la muerte tocando sus graves
    guitarras.
Oh España, qué triste pareces.

Also, the impersonal voice which reports, in "Reportaje," observes fullness (of life and time) as: ("Caminos / exteriores que otros andan.)" Those "other" in parenthesis may well be societies other than Spain.

In addition, in Hierro's next book, *Cuanto sé de mí* (1957), we find the impersonal, heart-rending lament ("llanto por . . .," as Spanish puts it) for Spain's Civil War exiles:

> Manuel del Río, natural
> de España, ha fallecido el sábado
> 11 de mayo, a consecuencia
> de un accidente. Su cadáver
> está tendido en D'Agostino
> Funeral Home. Haskell. New Jersey.

Compared with Hierro, Celaya is much more of a social poet. He believed that "La Poesía no es un fin en sí. La Poesía es un instrumento, entre otros, para transformar el mundo." But, as has been noted, "social" in Celaya is a euphemism "para designar esa mezcla de indignación, asco y vergüenza que uno experimenta ante la realidad en que vive" (Marco, *Siglo XX* 129-30). Celaya's *Cantos Iberos* (1955) lament the divisive poverty of post-Civil War Spain. In "A Sancho Panza," his demystification of the legend of "Don Quijote," he writes:

> Sancho-claro, Sancho-recio,
> Sancho que vistes las cosas como son y te callaste,
> metiendo el hombro, tratando
> de salvarnos del derrumbe con tu no lírico esfuerzo.
>
> Hombre a secas, Sancho-patria, pueblo-pueblo,
> pura verdad, fiel contraste
> de los locos que te explotan para vivir del recuerdo,
> ¡ya ha llegado tu momento!

Blas de Otero, who began as a religious poet and who evolved into a "poeta desarraigado," is as politically and socially committed as Celaya. In his "Cartilla (poética)," which begins, "La poesía tiene sus derechos," he exclaimed: "Ah las palabras más maravillosas, / 'rosa', 'poema', 'mar', / son *m* pura y otras letras: / o, a . . ." Then in "A la inmensa minoría" — from *Pido la paz y la palabra* (1955) — he wrote, "Yo doy todos mis versos por un hombre / en paz."

Angela Figuera is a strong social poet. Overlooked until recently, her *Obras completas* have just been published (by Hiperión). For example, *Belleza cruel* contains a satire on the notion of "Libertad" in the Spain of the day; and the book's title poem describes the horror and guilt the poet feels:

> cuando contemplo el rostro y el vestido
> de tantos hombres con el miedo al hombro,
> de tantos hombres con el hambre a cuestas,
> de tantas frentes con la piel quemada
> por la escondida rabia de la sangre.

Though the dominant trend in Spanish poetry of the late forties and early fifties is poetry with a socially committed tone, there are other important currents — somewhat overlooked — which run counter to that trend. In the first place, account must be taken of Vicente Aleixandre's post-surrealist work. In 1944 he published *Sombra del paraíso*, a book of immense subsequent influence, and one that provides a clear indication of what is seen as the *neo-romantic* current in post-Civil War Spanish poetry; its "Sierpe de amor" concludes:

> Entre tus pechos vivos levemente mi forma
> deslizaría su beso sin fin, como una lengua,
> cuerpo mío infinito de amor que día a día
> mi vida entera en tu piel consumara.

In the second place, there is the *postista* movement. *Postismo* is the heir to all "ismos" (and hence, *post*-ismo) of the twenties and thirties; it published its first manifesto in 1945. In the experimental work of Carlos Edmundo de Ory (b. 1923), Juan-Eduardo Cirlot (1916-73), and Miguel Labordeta (1921-69) much more autonomy is given to the image itself, and dream and surrealism are important elements.[8] In the third place, there is the "Grupo Cántico," from Córdoba, whose most well-known member is Ricardo Molina (1917-68), which cultivated a neo-romantic, sensual and baroque form of poetry.[9]

III. Mid 1950s to Mid 1960s

In the early 1960s, anthologizers again detected a new wave in Spanish poetry, in which the voices of the social critic seemed less important than those of the skeptic.[10] The poets of this group were adolescents during the Civil War. Hence, the War and its aftermath marked their lives and their early work. Though their poetry has social overtones, it is less *engagé* than that of a Celaya or an Otero; it is more concerned with the aridness and limitations for human existence in the latter half of the twentieth century. There is an ongoing debate amongst members of this group as to whether poetry is social communication between human beings — as suggested by Aleixandre and formulated by Bousoño — or whether it is "conocimiento," knowledge of specific psychic states — as Valente maintains.[11]

Of the great number of poets associated with this group the following stand out: Angel González (b. 1925), J.M. Caballero Bonald (b. 1926), Carlos Barral (b. 1928), José Agustín Goytisolo (b. 1928), Jaime Gil de Biedma (b. 1929), José Angel Valente (b. 1929), Francisco Brines (b. 1932), Claudio Rodríguez (b. 1934), Félix Grande (b. 1937), and Carlos Sahagún (b. 1938). A recent study (n. 11) of these poets called them "la segunda generación poética de posguerra," but frequently they are referred to as the poets of the 50s. Of these, the work of González, Gil de Biedma, Valente, Brines, Rodríguez, and Grande receives most attention.[12]

Angel González's early view of the world as "áspero" stems from inner disgruntlement: "Para vivir un año es necesario / morirse muchas veces mucho." He treats with contempt and sarcasm the peaks of modern, urban living; for example, in "Civilización de la opulencia" we find: "Particular mención merecen las vitrinas / donde se exhiben modas de señora." Since the late 60s, González's poetry displays even more irony and humor. In a series of linguistically inventive poems, he has shown himself to be a healthy demystifier of our society — and of poetry itself.

Gil de Biedma's is a more reflective and meditative verse. His poetic persona experiences people as soulless ("desenterrados vivos"). His *Moralidades* had deep repercussions in its explorations of what small pleasures there are in life. In it, childhood ("mundo abreviado, renovado y puro") and love are found to be important:

— Junto al cuerpo que anoche me gustaba
tanto desnudo, déjame que encienda
la luz para besarse cara a cara,
    en el amanecer.
Porque conozco el día que me espera,
    y no por el placer.

Gil de Biema's sardonic vision offers little hope of fulfillment: "envejecer, morir, / es el único argumento de la obra" (from *Poemas póstumos* [1968]).

José Angel Valente, a keen observer and critic of Western culture, has developed into a philosophical poet concerned with spiritual emptiness. In his first book, *A modo de esperanza* (1955), he defines, in "La rosa necesaria," by distinguishing his goal from that of Juan Ramón Jiménez, the type of beauty he believes a poet should seek in today's world:

21

La rosa que se aísla
en una mano, no;
la rosa
connatural al aire
que es de todos.

In *Poemas a Lázaro* (1960), his wit and philosophical questioning are mixed with doses of skepticism: "no debo / proclamar mi dolor . . . ¿qué salvación podré engendrar con un lamento?" In Valente, a continual reflection on whether life has any meaning is coupled with a desire to find something of value within the vast culture we have inherited: "Un poeta debe ser más útil / que ningún ciudadano de su tribu" (from *Breve son* [1968]).

Francisco Brines is a meditative poet — reminiscent of Cernuda. He is preoccupied with lost innocence: "Y abatimos / el árbol, derribamos la espesura / fresca de las palomas, la colina / donde se quedan las estrellas solas" (from *Las brasas* [1960]). The persona Brines projects is that of an outsider who is conscious that love must pass, but who finds — like Darío — that he must "insist" on the bitter truth poetry can articulate:

Hay en mi tosca taza un divino licor
que apuro y que renuevo:
desasosiega, y es
    remordimiento;
tengo a concubina a la virtud.
No tuve amor a las palabras,
¿cómo tener amor a vagos signos
cuyo desvelamiento era tan sólo
despertar la piedad del hombre para consigo mismo?
(*Insistencias en Luzbel* [1977])

Claudio Rodríguez's is the most affirmative voice in this group of poets. His early work foregrounds the surprises ("gifts," "inspiration") that are to be found in everyday living:

Todo es nuevo quizá para nosotros.
El sol claroluciente, el sol de puesta,
muere; el que sale es más brillante y alto
cada vez, es distinto, es otra nueva
forma de luz, de creación sentida.
Así cada mañana es la primera.
Para que la vivamos tú y yo solos,
nada es igual ni se repite.
(*Don de la ebriedad* [1953])

22

A similar basic belief is found in "A mi ropa tendida," published in *Conjuros* (1958). With *Alianza y condena* (1965), however, a more conflicted version is articulated: "¿Cómo sin la verdad / puede existir la dicha? He aquí todo."

In Félix Grande's work there is anguish. In "Sombra de sombra," from his first book, *Las piedras* (1964), he tells his persona: "Estorbas. Este mundo, hermoso para muchos, / iracundo te mira, te tiene hambre. Es cierto / que sobras, lo decían todos, y lo proclamas / tú mismo en la amargura tozuda de tus versos." However, in "Madrigal" he clings to the poetic word: "Eres una cerilla para mí, como ésa / que enciende por la noche y con la luz que vierte / alcanzo a ir a la cama viendo un poco, como ésa; / sin ti, sería tan duro llegar hasta la muerte." This desperation continues in *Música amenazada* (1966) — "Hay seres cuya vida se asemeja / a la de esa polvorienta y modesta bombilla / del cuarto inhabitado de la casa" — and also in "Puedo escribir los versos más tristes esta noche." However, with *Las Rubáiyátas de Horacio Martín* (1978), a deeper pleasure is extolled in sensual encounters.

IV. Mid 1960s to Mid 1970s

In 1970 an anthology appeared which signaled the arrival of another wave in contemporary Spanish poetry, a wave that subsequent anthologies have described in better and more impartial detail. This is the work of poets born after the Civil War, who first began to publish in the late 60s. They are referred to as the "Novísimos" and are distinguishable from previous generations because they eschew poetry of any political or social intent. Also, they derive some of their inspiration from non-traditional sources (cinema, mass media), as well as from different foreign poets (Pound, Eliot, Saint John Perse, Stevens, Octavio Paz, Lezama Lima). Among Spanish poets, they prefer Aleixandre, Lorca, and Cernuda. Although various anthologies have included almost one hundred poets with this group,[13] today the following stand out: Antonio Martínez Sarrión (b. 1939), Manuel Vázquez Montalbán (b. 1939), Antonio Carvajal (b. 1943), Justo Jorge Padrón (b. 1943), Félix de Azúa (b. 1944), Pere Gimferrer (b. 1945), Pureza Canelo (b. 1944), Antonio Colinas (b. 1946), Jenaro Talens (b. 1946), Guillermo Carnero (b. 1947), Leopoldo María Panero (b. 1948), Luis Alberto de Cuenca (b. 1950), Jaime Siles (b. 1951), and Luis Antonio de Villena (b. 1951).[14]

Like their predecessors, these poets reveal a preference for free verse and for the autonomy of the poetic image. Though their work is diverse (compare Vázquez Montalbán with Siles), it can tend toward the surreal and is highly estheticized. In fact, they have come to be labelled *culturalistas*, or the *escuela veneciana*, because of their fre-

23

quent intertextual references to Western culture in itself (especially to Grecian and to *fin-de-siècle* themes and movements).[15] This can be a highly experimental poetry, which also undermines late twentieth-century values.

The output of this group is immense, but particular notice has been taken of: Vázquez Montalbán's *Una educación sentimental* (1967), for its colloquial tone and cultural diversity; Gimferrer's *Arde el mar* (1966), for the breadth of its concerns; Carnero's *Dibujo de la muerte* (1971), for its mordant vision of post-modern Western culture; and Colinas's *Sepulcro en Tarquina* (1975), for its *culturalista* blend of quotidian and eternal cultures. The work of Panero has caused a stir for its *malditismo*,[16] and that of Siles for its classical learning and inclination toward "poesía pura."

V. Mid 1970s to Mid 1980s

In 1980 the *Premio Adonais* was awarded to a collection of poems by a very young woman; that in itself was presumably meant to signify something. The woman was Blanca Andreu, who was born in 1959, and the book, *De una niña de provincias que se vino a vivir en un Chagall*. Andreu's style is both surreal and baroque, in which respect she seems to continue the *culturalismo* of the "novísimos." However, in Andreu's preoccupations a reader can detect a movement toward a poetry that is concerned with the self and its psyche, that is, away from *culturalismo* and toward *intimismo*.

Andreu is one of a number of women poets who are important in Spanish poetry today. Amparo Amorós (*Ludía* [1983]) and Ana Rossetti (*Indicios vehementes* [1985]) are the two other major figures. Their work is vastly different. Rossetti is baroque, erotic, and skeptically humorous, whereas Amorós insists on a "rhetoric of silence" — implying that poems allude to a state of pre-lapsarian silence. If this is so, her poetics will take her in a completely different direction from the "novísimos" and their *culturalismo* (which implies that poetry is caught in the prison house of language, of *différance*).

Andreu's work and the Adonais prize gave prominence to the impact women are having on Spanish poetry today. In late 1985 an anthology appeared, *Las diosas blancas* (again from Hiperión) which brought many more women poets to the fore, some of whom are now publishing their first books: Margarita Arroyo, Lola Castro, María Luz Escuin, Menchu Gutiérrez, Almadena Guzmán, María del Carmen Pallarés, Lola Salinas, Lola Velasco. The tendency of this work is *intimista* rather than *culturalista*; it can be testimonial with a *neoromantic* concern with love and death.[17]

Although only a few women have found their way into the anthologies that have appeared, numerous young male poets have had

24

their work included.[18] This group is being called the "posnovísimos," but only time will tell just how different they are, if at all, from the "novísimos" themselves.

Despite this, it does seem from today's perspective that, in the late sixties with the "novísimos," a "tercera generación poética" emerged into Spanish poetry. It is, of course, still too soon to say if a fourth poetic generation began to emerge in the early eighties, with the latest wave of Spanish poets, the "posnovísmos."

NOTES

[1] Indispensable introductions to this period have been provided by: Joaquín Marco, "La poesía," *Historia crítica de la literatura española; Época contemporánea: 1939-1980,* ed. Domingo Ynduráín (Barcelona: Crítica, 1980) 109-38; Emilio Miró, "La poesia desde 1936," *Historia de la literatura española. IV. El siglo XX* (Madrid: Taurus, 1980) 327-89; and Fanny Rubio and José Luis Falcó, *Poesía española contemporánea (1939-1980)* (Madrid: Alhambra, 1981). For its clarity, the reader can profitably consult Ricardo Velilla's introduction to *Poesía española 1939-75: Antología* (Tarragona: Tarraco, 1977). Marco's essay was extended into a book, which does contain some useful clarifications on the original chapter: *Poesía española Siglo XX* (Barcelona: Edhasa, 1986).

Within the scope of the present brief survey, it is not possible to attend to the poetry written by Spaniards in exile. Women expatriates include Nuria Balcells (or Parés), Ernestina de Champourcin, Concha Méndez. Among the men, account would have to be given of: Antonio Aparicio, Manuel Durán, León Felipe, Pedro Grafias, Juan Gil-Albert, Francisco Giner de los Ríos, Juan Rejano, Luis Ríus, Adolfo Sánchez Vazquez, Arturo Serrano-Plaja, Tomás Segovia. See Miró (337-44).

[2] The following poets are also included in the anthology edited by Luis Jiménez Martos, *La generación poética de 1936* (Barcelona: Plaza & Janés, 1972): Juan Alcaide (1907-50), Enrique Azcoaga (1912), Guillermo Díaz-Plaja (1909-86), Pedro García Cabrera (1905), Fernando Gutiérrez (1911), Federico Muelas (1910) José Antonio Muñoz Rojas (1909), Carlos Rodríguez Spiteri (1911), Félix Ros (1912), Rafael Santos Torroella (1914). The name of Juan Ruiz Peña (1915) is also found with this group.

[3] The prior generation – of the 1920s – was associated with Góngora and the baroque. For the best account of this period, consult: Víctor García de la Concha, *La poesía española de posguerra* (Madrid: Prensa Española, 1973); the latter discusses the following features of *garcilasismo*: interest in the poetry of the "cancioneros," in neoplatonic love verse of the Renaissance, in the landscape of Castille as emblematic of the soul, in the decadent romanticism of J.R. Jiménez's *Arias tristes* and *Pastorales*, and in a superficially religious and confessional verse.

[4] Changes in Hernández's style can be glimpsed from the following examples. From *Perito:* "Agrios huertos, azules limonares, / de frutos, si dorados, / corredores; / ¡tan distantes!, que os sé si los vapores / libertan siempre presos

25

palomares." From *El rayo*: "Yo quiero ser llorando el hortelano / de la tierra que ocupas y estercolas, / compañero del alma, tan temprano." From *Viento*: "He poblado tu vientre de amor y sementera, / he prolongado el eco de sangre a que respondo / y espero sobre el surco como el arado espera: / he llegado al fondo." From *El hombre*: "Las cárceles se arrastran por la humedad del mundo, / van por la tenebrosa vía de los juzgados; / buscan a un hombre, buscan a un pueblo, lo persiguen, / lo absorben, se lo tragan."

[5]Francisco Ribes, *Antología consultada de la joven poesía española* (Valencia: Marés, 1952); Rafael Millán, *Veinte poetas españoles* (Madrid: Agora, 1955); Luis Jiménez Martos, *Nuevos poetas españoles* (Madrid: Agora, 1961); José María Castellet, *Veinte años de poesía española (1939-59)* (Barcelona: Seix Barral, 1962) and *Un cuarto de siglo de poesía española (1939-64)* (Barcelona: Seix Barral, 1966); Leopoldo de Luis, *Poesía social española contemporánea. 1939-68* (Madrid: Júcar, 1965).

[6]Other poets associated with this group include: María Beyneto (1925), Luis López Anglada, Salustiano Masó (1923), Agustín Millares Sall (1917), Antonio Molina (1927), Manuel Pacheco (1919), Salvador Pérez Valiente (1919).

[7]These comments do not do justice to the diversity of the poetry. The anthology of Leopoldo de Luis (n. 5) should be consulted with Francisco Ribes, *Poesía última* (Madrid: Taurus, 1975). See also: Félix Grande, *Apuntes sobre poesía española de posguerra* (Madrid: Taurus, 1970), and Julia Uceda's introduction to *José Luis Hidalgo: Antología poética* (Madrid: Aguilar, 1960).

[8]They were not known because until recently their work was hardly available. For example, Ory's *Metanoia* appeared in Cátedra in 1978 edited by Rafael de Cózar. Other *postistas* include: Juan Alcaide (1907-50), Gabino Alejandro Carriedo (1923), Eduardo Chicharro (1915-64), Antonio Fernández Molina (1927), Manuel Pinilla (1914); Gloria Fuertes (1917) and Angel Crespo (1926) are said to spring from *postismo*. See Marco, *Siglo XX* 133-36. Miró (359-61) notes that the *postistas* are "poetas malditos" who insisted that poetry is in touch with madness and darkness, and that therefore they were silenced during the Franco years.

[9]Other poets include: Manuel Alvarez Ortega (1923), Pablo García Baena (1923), Juan Bernier (1911), Julio Mariscal (1925-77). See Marco, *Siglo XX* (136-37).

[10]Originally the anthologies concerned were those of Ribes (see n. 7), Castellet (n. 5), and Jiménez Martos (n. 5). Subsequently, we have had: J. García Hortelano, *El grupo poético de los años 50* (Madrid: Taurus, 1978) and Antonio Hernández, *Los poetas del cincuenta. Una promoción desheredada* (Zaragoza: Zero-Zyx, 1978).

[11]For details: José Luis García Martín, *La segunda generación poética de la posguerra* (Badajoz: Depto. de Publicaciones de la Excma. Diputación, 1986) 88-97.

[12]Valente, González, Gil de Biema, Goytisolo, Caballero Bonald, and Barral frequented each other's company in Barcelona: they are sometimes called the "Grupo de la Colección Collioure" (the town in southern France where Machado died). Others – Brines, Rodríguez, Sahagún – published their first work with Adonais and have been called the "Grupo de Adonais."

For editions of the work of those cited in the text, consult. F. Brines, *Poesía 1960-81* (Madrid: Visor, 1984); A. González, *Palabra sobre palabra* (Barcelona: Seix Barral, 1986); F. Grande, *Biografía. Poesía completa (1958-84)* (Barcelona: Anthropos, 1986); C. Rodríguez, *Desde mis poemas* (Madrid: Cátedra, 1983); and J.A. Valente, *Punto Cero: Poesía 1953-79* (Barcelona: Seix Barral, 1980).

The following poets are also associated with this wave of poetry: Manuel Alcántara (1928), Carlos Alvarez (1933), Elena Andrés, María Victoria Atencia (1931), Enrique Badosa (1927), Eladio Cabañero (1930), Alfonso Canales (1923), Alfonso Costafreda (1926), Angel Crespo (1926), Juan José Cuadros (1927), J.B. de Luca (1934), Concha de Marco, Aquilino Duque, Jaime Ferrán (1928), J. Folch (1926-48), A. García Calvo (1931), L. Gomis (1924), Rafael Guillén (1933), María Elvira Lacaci (1929?), Concha Lagos, Jesus Lizano (1931), A.G. Lomis (1935), Jesus López Pacheco (1930), Manuel Mantero (1930), Joaquín Marco (1935), J. Mariscal Montes (1925), José Luis Martín Descalzo (1930), Elena Martín Vivaldi, Rafael Montesinos (1920), Carlos Murciano (1931), Pilar Paz Pasamar, J.L. Pardo Noguiera (1919), Mariano Roldán (1932), R. Soto Vergés (1936), Julia Uceda (1928).

[13]The original, controversial anthology is by J.M. Castellet, *Nueve novísimos poetas españoles* (Barcelona: Barral, 1970). See also: José Batlló, *Poetas españoles poscontemporáneos* (Barcelona: El Bardo, 1974); José Luis García Martín, *Las voces y los ecos* (Madrid: Júcar, 1980); C.G. Moral and R.M. Pereda, *Joven poesía española* (Madrid: Cátedra, 1980); and E. de Jongh Rossel, *Florilegium: Poesía última española* (Madrid: Espasa Calpe, 1982).

[14]The following poets are associated with the "novísimos": Isabel Abad, Alejandro Amusco, José María Alvarez (1942), Juan Barja (1951), Marcos Ricardo Barnatán (1946), José Batlló (1939), Francisco Bejarano (1945), Juan Manuel Bonet (1944), Víctor Botas (1945), Joaquín Caro Romero (1940), Carlos Clementson (1944), Pedro J. de la Peña (1944), Miguel D'Ors (1946), Augustin Delgado (1941), Gloria Diez (1949), Javier Egea, José Elías (1941), Baltasar Espinosa (1937), Angel Fierro (1941), J.L. García Martín, José Luis Giménez Frontín (1940), Antonio Hernández (1943), Mario Hernández (1945), Ramón Irigoyen (1942), Diego Jesús Jiménez (1942), Julio López, Armando López Castro (1949), Aurora Luque, Fernando Millán (1944), César A. Molina (1952), Vicente Molina Foix (1946), Jesús Moreno Sánz (1949), Enrique Morón (1942), Jesús Muñarriz (1940), Manuel Neila (1950), Anibal Núñez, Fernando Ortiz (1947), Victor Pozanco (1940), Pedro Provencio (1943), Ignacio Prat (1945-81), José A. Ramírez Lozano (1950), Miguel Ramos, Florinda Salinas, Alvaro Salvador (1950), Mariano Sánchez, Eloy Sánchez Rosillo (1948), Luis Suñén, José Miguel Ullán (1944), Jorge Urrutia (1945).

[15]They are also called "del sándalo" (as opposed to "la berza"), and "del lenguaje." Theirs is an intellectual poetry in which Western culture (literature, music, history) plays a part in helping the poetic persona in its metaphysical exploration of reality. Hence, metapoetic, neoclassic, and neobaroque elements abound. For clarification, see: M.A. Gómez Segade et al., "Rumbos de la poesía española en los ochenta," *ALEC* 9.1-3 (1984): 175-200, esp. 184.

[16]Allusions to drugs, to the sensual human body, and to hetero and homosexual activites are found in some of the "novísimos." See Gómez Segade (n. 15) 185.

[17]José Olivio Jiménez, "Reafirmación, Proximidad, Continuidad: Notas hacia la poesía española última (1975-85)," *Las nuevas letras* 3-4 (1985): 40-48, has observed that, in comparison to the earlier group, the most recent poets seem to be putting less distance between their work and life itself (47).

[18]The following poets are also referred to as "posnovísimos." The distinction between "novísimo" and "posnovísimo" seems to be whether they were born between 1955 and 1960, or whether they published their first book after 1980: Emilio Barón (1954), Fernando Beltrán (1956), Felipe Benítez (1960), Carmen Borja, José M. Cabra de Luna, José Carlón (1954), Juan Carlos Castaño (1954), Julia Castillo (1956), Bernd Dietz (1953), Antonio Enrique (1952), Carlos Farraco (1952), Luis García Montero (1958), Juan Garzón (1954), Jose Gutiérrez (1955), Miguel Herráez, José Luis Jover, Abelardo Linares (1952), Salvador López Becerra (1957), Lostalé, José Lupiáñez (1955), Julio Alonso Llamazares (1955), L. Martínez Merlo, Miguel Más (1955), Justo Navarro (1953), Carlos Piera (1942), Vicente Presa (1952), Pedro Provencio, Vicente Sabido (1953), Manuel Sánchez Chamorro (1954), Antonio Sánchez Robayna (1952), E. Sánchez Rosillo, Rafael Suárez Ortiz (1956), Andrés Trapiello (1953), and Miguel Velasco.

The reader who wants a sample of "Poesía última: 1987" may consult *El Urogallo* 12 (1987): 35-50. It contains a selection of fifteen poets who are now in their twenties and whose names are new. *El País*'s book review for "12 de marzo, 1987" also contains interesting critical comments.

THREE MOMENTS OF
POST-CIVIL WAR SPANISH POETRY

Andrew P. Debicki
The University of Kansas

Any attempt to define the poetic currents of a forty-year period of history forces one to make dangerous generalizations; an attempt to define such currents in post-Civil War Spanish poetry also forces one to deal with questionable generalizations made by earlier critics. In order to construct a useful and hopefully somewhat novel overview, while avoiding such dangerous generalizations, I will attempt to focus my comments on one main issue: the way in which three successive moments and generations of post-War poetry introduced and exemplified new ways of exploiting language. I will explore this issue through the analysis of a few specific texts, hoping in this fashion to bring some precision to my points.

Standard interpretations of Spanish post-Civil War poetry begin by noting the formalism of the early 1940s; the salient poets of this period, most of them connected with the magazine *Garcilaso*, produced serene, skillful, but mostly intranscendent verse, written in traditional forms and focused on nostalgic love, an admiration of nature, and well-controlled religious feelings. The first significant period of post-War poetry is marked by the appearance of the magazine *Espadaña* and of Dámaso Alonso's *Hijos de la ira* in 1944, and by the subsequent unfolding of social and existential currents in Spanish verse. *Espadaña*, as critics have noted, was dominated by poets concerned with social issues and with the problems of daily life in Franco's Spain.[1] It was published until 1951. Somewhat later, in the early 1950s, Blas de Otero, Gabriel Celaya, and others published books dealing with social issues and written in everyday language, and gained a wide reading public. The social and "realistic" current of the late 1940s and early 1950s is apparent when one examines the two main anthologies of the period, the *Antología consultada de la joven poesía española* and Rafael Millán's *Veinte poetas españoles*.

The other main current of the time is an existential one. Alonso's *Hijos de la ira*, much of Victoriano Crémer's work, and some of Otero's deal with the anguish of individuals living in a hostile, often meaningless environment. The poetry of Carlos Bousoño reveals a questioning search for some reality beyond illusions; the early work of José Hierro deals with the impact of time on human life and searches for understanding in the face of surrounding enigmas. The existentialist and neoromantic current of post-War poetry is another facet of the impulse to "rehumanize" verse and bring it into consonance with the preoccupations of the times.

Vicente Aleixandre, in a speech delivered in 1955, summarized very well the main features of Spanish poetry of this period: "El tema esencial de la poesía de nuestros días es . . . el cántico del hombre en cuanto *situado*, es decir en cuanto *localizado*; localizado en un tiempo, en un tiempo que pasa y es irreversible, y localizado en un espacio, en una sociedad determinada, con unos determinados problemas que le son propios."[2] This tendency of poetry to be "situated" would account not only for social verse (situated in the immediate problems of Spain) and existential writings (situated in the preoccupations of its time), but also for other important works of the era: Alexandre's own *Sombra del paraíso*, with its stress on the emotive and irrational aspects of human existence; Luis Rosales' *La casa encendida*, dominated by subjective visions of reality; Leopoldo Panero's *Escrito a cada instante*, which uses private remembrances to point to larger issues. It is very important to note, with Carlos Bousoño, that in this period the issue of generations and the ages of the poets plays a minimal role: under the impact of given circumstances, poets of different ages produce very similar works.[3]

All these characteristics led José María Castellet, in 1960, to speak of a whole new era of direct and realistic poetry which would mark the end of the more universal and stylized tradition that had come down from the Symbolists and reached its culmination in the works of the Generation of the 1920s.[4] From our perspective, however, such an overview seems too facile; having read the later works of Angel González and Gloria Fuertes, we know that the use of colloquial language and the presence of social themes do not imply lack of poetic skill or of universality. Knowing poems of the 1970s which present social concerns in highly elaborate and artistic fashion, we reject an automatic opposition between commitment and aesthetic concerns. All of this invites us to take a new look at the poetry of the first post-War period.

When we do so, and look again at the colloquial language used by the poets of the time, we quickly see that it is often handled with great artistry, destroying any notion that poetry written with everyday expressions is less aesthetically valuable than any other. We do, however, discover new ways of using language creatively, combined with new attitudes regarding its function, and come to realize that these underlie not only the best poetry of the first post-War period but much of the poetry written later by writers as different as Claudio Rodríguez, Angel González, Gloria Fuertes, Guillermo Carnero, Pere Gimferrer, and Antonio Colinas. Instead of drawing an opposition between artistic pre-War poetry and realistic post-War verse, we can then begin to examine these new ways of creating meaning through language that emerge in the post-War period, and continue to evolve to our days, and their implications.

Some of these are apparent in "Insomnio," the first poem in Dámaso Alonso's *Hijos de la ira*:

> Madrid es una ciudad de más de un millón de cadáveres
> (según las últimas estadísticas).
> A veces en la noche yo me revuelvo y me incorporo en
> este nicho en el que hace 45 años que me pudro,
> y paso largas horas oyendo gemir el huracán, o ladrar
> los perros, o fluir blandamente la luz de la luna.
> Y paso largas horas gimiendo como el huracán, ladrando
> como un perro enfurecido, fluyendo como la leche
> de la ubre caliente de una gran vaca amarilla.
> Y paso largas horas preguntándole a Dios, preguntándole
> por qué se pudre lentamente mi alma,
> por qué se pudren más de un millón de cadáveres en
> esta ciudad de Madrid,
> por qué mil millones de cadáveres se pudren lentamente
> en el mundo.
> Dime, ¿qué huerto quieres abonar con nuestra
> podredumbre?
> ¿Temes que se te sequen los grandes rosales del día,
> las tristes azucenas letales de tus noches?[5]

The poem is based on a very specific historical reality; written in 1940, when Alonso was in his early 40's, it refers to the fact that Madrid's population had reached a million. It adopts, at the outset, a prosaic tone: its first line imitates a newspaper report, and we begin to read it without paying much attention. The word "cadáveres," of course, breaks this tone, forcing us to see the statement as image rather than news item. This word also introduces a series of references to death: if the inhabitants of Madrid are cadavers, the speaker sleeps in a niche, his life has been a long dying ("me pudro"), and all humans are cadavers. Thus the supposedly prosaic reality with which the poem began is extended into metaphor and into allegory, and the poem conveys not a literal fact but a subjective vision of life's meaninglessness. Yet much of the impact of the metaphorical pattern comes from the way in which it rises up, surprisingly and dramatically, out of an everyday expression and reality.

In lines three and four, the poem evokes the traditions of Romantic poetry. Sleepless and anguished, the speaker listens to the hurricane and the dogs, watches the moonlight, and then echoes Nature's emotions in line four. Every detail evokes a commonplace of Romantic poetry, until the reference to the "warm udder of a big yellow cow" undercuts and parodies them all. If lines one and two led us from literal statement to allegorical vision, lines three and four carry us from a Romantic declaration of anguish back to a parody and a very literal-minded description.

It is important to note that this process takes place amidst intertextual echoes. The images of line three evoke, as I noted, the traditions of Romantic poetry; the specific view of Madrid as a cemetery recalls, as Philip Silver has noted, a well-known work of Larra.[6] Line one, as indicated, evokes statements made in Madrid newspapers in 1940.

But how does all of this demonstrate a new way of approaching language? The poem's tone and vocabulary are admittedly more colloquial than those of much poetry of the 1920s; but metaphorical patterns and intertextualities have been the staples of poetry for a long time, and even the use of a speaker developing his insights in a dramatic monologue can be traced back at least as far as Browning. Yet there is something fundamentally new and different in this text. The various elements present — the journalistic declaration, the sustained metaphor of the cadaver, the romantic anguish, the parodic image of the cow — do not fit together in the way in which the elements of a typical poem of the 1920s do. Instead, they seem to form a heterogeneous combination of several levels of discourse, much in the way that a collage combines several layers of picture surface. The speaker, of course, gives unity to all these materials and uses them all to convey his sense of alienation (the metaphor of the cemetery and the romantic allusions point to his anguish, while the modern tone and parody underline his modern setting and his ability to laugh at himself). But the text itself remains a mixture of diverse modes of expression and in this way differs from a classic poem of the Symbolist tradition.

By thus combining diverse modes of expression, "Insomnio" at least implicitly challenges a fundamental premise of the Symbolist tradition (and of traditional analytic criticism as well): that a literary work is a cohesive structure, containing within itself, in static form, a set repository of meanings. In contrast to, for example, Guillén's "Perfección," "Insomnio" does not embody, in well-coordinated words and images, a single experience. Rather it uses its combination of layers of language to make the reader sense, in diverse ways, the vision of a society and a speaker in crisis.

The implications of this process become even clearer as we take into account the rest of the poem. The speaker's questioning of God picks up the image of rottenness, but also inserts it into the tradition of a Biblical lament and, more specifically, of the Book of Job (the parallel long lines intensify the evocation). The suggested meaning for human life as fertilizer for God's garden on the one hand makes existence extremely limited, but on the other points to what will be a central theme of all of *Hijos de la ira*, the need for Man to become more passive and accepting of life. The poem thus continues fanning out in several directions, held together only by the speaker's anguish and the general theme of a search for meaning among negative surroundings.

One could object that the differences I have noted between this poem and a traditional Symbolist work simply constitute the insertion of techniques common to narrative fiction into poetry: point of view play, tone changes, a use of intertextualities to modify and put into question a speaker's perspective. This poem presents the initial attitude of the protagonist of *Hijos de la ira* and marks the beginning of his narrative, his complex quest for meaning amidst a chaotic world.[7] But even if all the diverse perspectives and levels of language in "Insomnio" can be explained as features of a narrative mode, they still move this text beyond poetry's traditional role as unmediated embodiment of experience through language — one of the basic characteristics attributed to the lyric in the Symbolist tradition.

I am not even sure that the diverse levels of the poem *are* resolved in the speaker's perspective and narrative. His central role as a modern-day romantic does not require the abrupt undercutting of romantic clichés with a parody, or the Biblical echoes, or the unusual intertextualities. The extreme nature of the language shifts, I would suggest, are directed more at the poem's reader than at a definition of its speaker or his story. These shifts invite the reader to step back from the text, to respond to it not as a single fictitious world but as a weaving together of diverse elements, all of which interact within the reader's own knowledge (his/her awareness of the trivialities of journalistic language, a recall of the lamentations of Romantic poetry, knowledge of the Bible, a view of the modern city). This produces a very different process of reading than does a cohesive Symbolist poem, or even a traditional novel. And yet it does not make "Insomnio" any less artful than an early Guillén poem — just different in its goals and its way of using language artistically.

This view of "Insomnio" invites us to reexamine other works published in the 1940s and early 1950s by authors of different ages. Blas de Otero's poetry, for example, acquires new dimensions: we will be able to relate some of its characteristics (its way of making new meanings out of clichés, its use of allusions and literary echoes, its surprising endings and ways of undercutting its own images — all features studied by Alarcos Llorach) to a new way of creating experience so as to involve the reader in its production. In a recent study, María Nowakowska Stycos has examined Otero's use of lines of poetry written by earlier writers, showing how these are altered and combined in a new setting.[8] Not only does this process call into question the nature of a work's "originality" (which cannot reside in the lines of poetry themselves, just in their interweaving), but it suggests that its meaning is expandable rather than static. Each reader will recall the lines from different authors in different ways, will bring in somewhat different contexts and "horizons of expectation," and will to some degree become a co-author of the poem/collage.

Likewise some of the poetry of Gabriel Celaya will reveal unsuspected dimensions; its frequent use of "system breakage" ("rupturas de sistema"), its juxtapositions of contrasting styles and tones, and its surprising combinations of concrete images and abstract themes seem evidence not of artistic carelessness or inability to construct a cohesive work, but of a new way of envisioning and executing a text.[9] (In connection with this, Celaya's idea that the essence of poetic language should be novelty and surprise, and the premium that he places in his essays on the importance of the reader's reactions, suddenly become an important clue to his verse and the whole period.)

All this is not to deny, of course, that much of the verse written in the first post-War period stays mired in its social message or its direct presentation of existential anguish. But we have tended to undervalue much good poetry of the period because we have demanded that it meet canons forged in the Symbolist tradition; a new perspective, one more accepting of the possibility of the text as a creative play of various levels of language and as a stimulus to the creative response of the reader, will let us discover much value that we have neglected. Our younger generation of critics, grounded in the structuralist and post-structuralist tradition of looking at *texts* and their possibilities rather than seeking the closure of poetic *works*, is in an ideal situation to undertake this process.[10]

Let us return to Aleixandre's idea that post-War poetry deals with Man as *situated* in his time and place. We had come to equate this focus with simplistic ideological postures and with crude social verse. But the best poetry of the period stands almost at an opposite extreme: by taking into account all of life's circumstances, by immersing itself in various levels of language, including the most colloquial, and in multiple perspectives on language and reality, and by involving the reader in its process of naming and discovery, it takes cognizance of Man's situation while it simultaneously opens up a vast area of possibilities for poetic creation.

It is also worth recalling an essay by Carlos Bousoño, written in 1961, in which he describes "postcontemporary" poetry, with clear reference to the first post-War period.[11] Taking into account the narrative nature of much of this poetry, its objectivism, and its use of anecdote, Bousoño suggests that this poetry places its author in a much less exalted position than that dictated by earlier, "contemporary" poetry (which would include the Generation of the 1920s), and ends up being less "individualistic." This fits in very well with my notion of its openness to the reader and supports the view that the first post-War period marks the beginning of a new poetic attitude which breaks with the Symbolist vision of the closed text. Despite significant changes in the themes and style that have taken place since then, this attitude extends down to the present.

The possibilities of a more open poetic language are further expanded in the next period of post-Civil War poetry, which I see as extending from the late 1950s through the 1960s and early 1970s. At this point, one can again speak of the appearance of a generation. Most of the significant new poets of this period were born between 1925 and 1938; they were children during the Civil War, they grew up amidst the stagnation of the Franco era, and they developed their writing at a time during which social themes and direct expression dominated poetic expression.[12] Their work obviously could not ignore the shift that had occurred in poetic language or slide back into a Symbolist poetic; it was their task, rather, to fully develop the artistic possibilities of everyday language, to create a poetry that would carry forward the discoveries of the first post-War period. In this task they were joined by several older poets who had already revealed their talent in the 1940s and 1950s, but whose work, to my mind, fits better the even more creative bent of the 1960s, for example, José Hierro, whose *Libro de las alucinaciones* came out in 1966, and Carlos Bousoño, whose poetry became extremely significant in the 60s and whose studies of the younger poets of the time contain very important insights into their work.

To fully appreciate this generation of poets, one must keep in mind their views on writing. Almost all of them emphasize the importance of poetry as an act of discovery. They place special stress on the fact that a poem's meaning emerges in the process of its composition, and does not constitute a previously established message. They also attribute a major role to the reader, who becomes a co-participant in the discovery of meanings. Enrique Badosa, rejecting the view of poetry as direct communication, writes: "En la poesía el poeta se conoce más a sí mismo y a las cosas, gracias a su poema, e — igual que le lector — tiene ocasión de hallarse en una nueva experiencia ..." José Angel Valente's formulation has become a classic statement of the generation's poetic: "Todo poema es, pues, una exploración de materia de experiencia no previamente conocida ... De ahí que el proceso de la creación poética sea un movimiento de indagación y tanteo en el que la identificación de cada nuevo elemento modifica a los demás ... porque todo poema es un conocimiento 'haciéndose'."[13]

This vision of poetry, as has been pointed out by many critics, sets the second post-War generation against the more utilitarian attitude taken by many social poets and marks a return to a more aesthetic vision. But, in another sense, it also continues and justifies the attitude to the poem as creative play and as a stimulus to the reader's response which we saw emerging in the previous period. It also carries forward Celaya's notion of poetic language as creating novelty and surprise. (The way in which the second generation's poetics builds on previous attitudes has not been noted, I suspect, because the earlier poets tended to pay lip service to a simplistic social view of art even when they transcended it in their works.) The new poetics of this time also stresses the importance of the word as *creating* rather than just conveying meaning; Claudio Rodríguez has stated this most succinctly: "Las palabras funcionan en el poema, no sólo con su natural capacidad de decir o significar, sino, además, en un grado fundamental, en el sentido de su actividad en el conjunto de los versos."14

The poetics of this second post-War generation, then, rationalizes and extends what I have suggested as the most important innovation of their immediate predecessors: the creation of texts which are not static and cohesive embodiments of previously forged meanings, but rather multi-layered explorations of human experience — explorations in which the reader is a participant as well as a receiver. The poetry of the second generation exemplifies this vision even more consistently, while revealing a uniformity of excellence superior to that of its predecessors. It demonstrates, to my mind, how diverse levels of language, from the colloquial to the elaborately referential, can be controlled, combined, and used effectively to create unique — and uniquely open — artistic experiences.

José Angel Valente's own poetry furnishes excellent examples. Margaret Persin has shown how many of Valente's poems juxtapose diverse codes of language to make his reader witness and share the very process of poetic creation; I have examined the way in which intertextualities produce conflicting visions in his work.15 In "Reaparición de lo heroico," for example, a seemingly reasonable outlook on life is undercut by our realization that the speaker is one of the suitors in the *Odyssey* and is attacking the whole tradition of heroism.

Many poems by Angel González illustrate even more dramatically the creative play of language so typical of this generation. Breaking the customary demarcations between different levels of expression, González presents a love declaration in the language normally used to order coffee in a restaurant in "Eso era amor" and — as Martha La Follette Miller has shown — makes cockroaches his equals in "Dato biográfico."16 Together with Gloria Fuertes, who constantly mixes levels of language to extend the limits of poetic discourse, González demonstrates the potential of poetry for calling into question both our normal ways of seeing reality and our normal ways of saying things about it.

The work of Claudio Rodríguez exemplifies very well the new use of language in post-War poetry. Several previous studies have already so indicated: Carlos Bousoño has demonstrated how Rodríguez's unique kind of allegory inverts the normal correspondences between real and metaphorical planes, Martha La Follette Miller has examined how metapoetic references take his poetry beyond mere representation of its subjects, and I have commented on ways in which a juggling of different language codes produces the sense of enigmatic experiences, which the reader is invited to confront but not resolve.[17] Rodríguez's poetry, in fact, may convey better than that of any other poet of his time the sense of multiplicity and mystery of human existence. Focused thematically on the conflict between various positive and negative forces of life (we immediately think of *alianza* and *condena*), it embarks on a search for transcendence, but makes the reader a participant rather than a mere witness, and its language a set of clues rather than an answer to the quest. We can see this exemplified in the poem "Hilando," from *El vuelo de la celebración*; the text, of course, refers explicitly to Valázquez's painting *Las hilanderas*:

(*La hilandera, de espaldas,*
del cuadro de Velázquez)

Tanta serenidad es ya dolor.
Junto a la luz del aire
la camisa ya es música, y está recién lavada,
aclarada,
bien ceñida al escorzo
risueño y torneado de la espalda,
con su feraz cosecha,
con el amanecer nunca tardío
de la ropa y la obra. Este es el campo
del milagro: helo aquí,
en el alba del brazo,
en el destello de estas manos, tan acariciadoras
devanando la lana,
el hilo y el ovillo,
y la nuca sin miedo, cantando su viveza,
y el pelo muy castaño
tan bien trenzado,
con su moño y su cinta;
y la falda segura, sin pliegues, color jugo de acacia.

Con la velocidad del cielo ido,
con el taller, con

37

el ritmo de las mareas de las calles,
está aquí, sin mentira,
con un amor tan mudo y con retorno,
con su celebración y con su servidumbre.[18]

The poem constitutes, on the most basic level, a celebration of and an homage to the art of Velázquez. Selecting one figure from Velázquez's painting, a weaver in its right foreground who works with her back to the viewer, Rodríguez focuses on the vivid effect which this figure produces. The image of her blouse as music, the description of her shoulder, and the whole portrayal of her hands weaving and of her being situated in a "campo / del milagro" (lines 9-10), convey to the reader the vividness of Velázquez's art, his surprising way of making its subjects seem alive. Yet we immediately note that the life-like quality of the figure is presented via constant references to its (and the painting's) artfulness: the work is a miracle, the figure is an "escorzo," the painting "sings" the woman's beauty, the blouse is "music." Presenting the scene as the never-delayed dawn of "ropa" and "obra" stresses its artistic timelessness (while combining in one phrase a concrete detail and a reference to the art object). In addition, the woman's actions, which come across as so life-like, involve weaving, the making of materials for art. Even her physical presence, with her braided hair and her ribbon, also points to a kind of artfulness. By thus playing off the artistic and the life-like, the poem immerses us in the whole theme of the relationships between the two.

This leads us back to the poem's puzzling first line, and its assertion "tanta serenidad es ya dolor." It could, of course, merely allude to the fact that the figure in the painting is both gracefully balanced and straining at her task. But the paradoxical linking of serenity and pain echoes, on some level, the conjunction of naturalness and artistry that dominates the text. One additional, seemingly insignificant detail catches our eye: the way in which line 3 dwells on the "camisa" as "recién lavada," right after using the image of music to convey its artistry. It recalls the poem "A mi ropa tendida" from Rodríguez's *Conjuros*, which used multiple perspectives to produce a tensive view of the theme of purification.[19] The intertextual echo (possibly accidental) is another way of mixing diverse levels of life and art.

The second stanza steps back from the details of the previous description and presents an overview of the woman's task and role. It includes allusions to elements not present in the painting ("cielo ido," "mareas de las calles"); it thus treats the woman as more than just a figure in that painting, as somehow real outside of it. This makes us wonder if the "celebración" and "servidumbre" that the poem's speaker sees projected in her are found only in her pictorial representation or are a part of her life beyond the painting? The demarcations between life and art have definitely been blurred, and the phrase "sin mentira" sounds very enigmatic in view of the puzzling lack of distinction between the two realms. What is the nature of this truth?

The poem never gives a definitive answer, leaving the reader to consider the whole question of the intertwining of life (and maybe life-like-ness) and art. In that sense, it exemplifies very well the open-ended text which I am suggesting is characteristic of post-War poetry. That does not imply lack of specific meanings: "Hilando" captures, through its words and vividness, various dimensions of the relationship of life and art. But it does not close them into a single tight vision, as would a typical poem of the Symbolist tradition.

"Hilando" does not use colloquial language in the way that "Insomnio," or a typical poem of Gabriel Celaya, or Angel González's "Eso era amor" do. But I would still call its language "post-Symbolist" and relate it to the mainstream of post-War poetry. Its vocabulary does not forge the sparse and cohesive closed world of a typical poem from Guillén's *Cántico*; its specific details and conversational tone immerse us in a mixed world of the painting's anecdote on the one hand and the theme of artistry on the other, inviting us to share and extend the speaker's sense of discovery. It thus exemplifies the way in which the poetry of the Generation of the 1950s uses language: situating us in a specific world, it involves us in a process of exploration in which elements modify each other and which results, to recall Valente's phrase, in a "conocimiento haciéndose."

The third moment of post-Civil War poetry is introduced by the appearance of José María Castellet's anthology *Nueve novísimos poetas españoles* in 1970.[20] Although there was an element of propagandistic exaggeration in Castellet's description of the appearance of a new poetry, the later writings of the major poets he introduced clearly confirm a new poetic sensibility. In very general terms, the work of these poets is stylistically complex, depends on literary as well as other allusions, and stands in contrast to the colloquial and narrative vein of the preceding periods. In an important study published as an introduction to Guillermo Carnero's *Ensayo de una teoría de la visión*, Carlos Bousoño stresses this new generation's aestheticism and individualism, its questioning of rationalist formulations and its distrust of the possibility of fully knowing reality through poetry, as well as the self-referential and metapoetic bent of much of its work.[21] For Bousoño, all these traits are related to a profound skepticism of traditional systems of knowing and to a sense of alienation ("marginación") from political institutions and social conventions.

All of these traits seem to separate this generation from earlier post-War poetry and link it back to modernism, to the vanguard movements of the early 1920s, and to the poetry of Guillén (in its creativity) and Cernuda (in its rebellious visions). A member of the generation, Pere Gimferrer, gives support to such a view when he attacks the intranscendent quality of realistic post-War poetry and calls attention to other post-War writers who had been ignored but who to him represent a link between the creativity of the 1920s and that of his own generation.[22] (These include the *Cántico* group of Córdoba and Carlos Edmundo de Ory.)

In one extremely significant way, however, this new generation continues a line that emerged in earlier post-War writing and that characterizes all Spanish poetry since that time. Its poetics and its poetry are grounded in a vision of the literary text as an open-ended system rather than a closed and fully explainable work. Gimferrer, Guillermo Carnero, and several of their contemporaries are more skeptical than their predecessors about the efficacy of poetic language in discovering reality (though we can already find some of that skepticism in Valente). These younger poets view the text as revealing only whatever reality it can build with words — which explains their metapoetic bent. This attitude, however, brings them to a view of poetry as creative play — a view which we already saw emerging in Dámaso Alonso's "Insomnio" and which was very apparent in the Generation of the 1950s. The echo of surrealism that we find in Gimferrer's generation is related to this vision of the poem. (It also suggests that its seeds can be found in some writings of 1915-1925, although they are barely perceptible in the dominant works of the Generation of the 1920s.)

This view of the third post-War generation is confirmed in many of its poems. Tim Rogers has studied the use of *collage* in Gimferrer's works, showing how multi-layered references to literary and pop culture combine to produce an exploration of language and life which "causes the reader to participate as co-creator in a poetic process which yields multiple readings."[23] In his comments on Carnero's *El sueño de Escipión*, Bousoño pins down how the poem brings into question the very realities it portrays, likening the process to the ways in which some painters cross out elements in their work to suggest their inadequacy (which in turn suggests a relation between the poetry and art of this period and the deconstructive vision of the sign "under erasure"). Bousoño illustrates how Carnero's poems undercut and modify the conventional meanings of the language they display and notes how they explore poetic language and its deformation of reality.[24]

A good example of the use of language by a younger poet is "Escena de caza" from the book *Ludia* by Amparo Amorós. The whole volume is centered on poetic perspective, on the ways in which language both can and cannot seize the essence and beauty of things. The poem I will discuss begins with a quotation from Ovid's *Metamorphoses*, setting the subject in a literary perspective. The quotation describes Daphne's flight from Apollo via the images of hound and hare, accenting the gracefulness of the action rather than its plot value. The text which follows then describes the scene as a work of art (and seems, in fact, to refer to a painting of the myth):

Lo primero que alcanza a percibir
el testigo ocasional,
antes de alzar la mano deteniendo
la imagen, con un gesto
del ágil antebrazo que sustenta
la señal enguantada,
es el bronco jadeo
de los mastines
que integran la jauría.

Levanta ya los párpados y observa
el sabio orden de los lugares
que cada bulto ocupa
en el rectángulo
del apresurado espacio.
La luz da a cada forma su volumen preciso.
Los límites definen las figuras
sobre un aire en tensión.
Un punto en el conjunto
atrae la mirada:
en él están implícitos la gracia,
el deseo acechante,
un zureo de duda,
la carrera, los cuerpos casi vuelo,
el sucederse en frágil equilibrio,
los materiales mismos de la obra,
el instante feliz y su contrario.

(— No ofendió con torpeza nuestras frentes
describiendo también los personajes —)

No podemos detener la belleza
más que un único instante
— piensa. Desciende el arco
que su brazo tensara unos segundos
y devuelve el tapiz al movimiento
asumiendo el peligro de la huida.[25]

The action referred to in the poem, the chase of Daphne by Apollo, is thus set back several levels from anecdotal reality; we first see it in a quotation from a poem, then as a visual work of art, and one contemplated by a seemingly detached observer. The picture is frozen at one point in time, and its aesthetic balance is stressed. Its value lies in the harmonious distribution of figures, in the play of light and volume, in the materials of the composition. Stanza three carries the stylization to an extreme, indicating that the observer avoids even the realistic intrusion of describing the characters.

And yet it is precisely this stylization which imparts vividness and an air of reality to the picture. The first thing the observer sees in the artistic scene is the panting of the dogs — an elemental act of life. As he contemplates the harmony of the objects before him, he becomes aware of the tension in the figures, the desire, the sense of movement in the bodies, the material presence of the picture. We remember, too, that the observer's perception of all this vividness occurs when he has stopped the image (lines 3-4), when he has artificially detained the flow of the story. His aesthetic detachment and the distancing of an artistic perspective have not impeded but rather engendered the vividness of life.

The last stanza begins with the observer's meditation on the impossibility of freezing beauty for long, which recalls his detached aestheticism. But when this observer now lets the action go on, we get a sense of life overwhelming art. We notice, too, that the observer's hand, which was raised to stop the action, is called an "arco / que su brazo tensara" when it is lowered to let life continue. Is it far-fetched to suggest that this evokes the picture of a bow ready to shoot an arrow and recalls the arrow shot by Cupid to start Apollo's pursuit of Daphne? Somehow, the vivid mythological story and the artistic contemplation and embodiment of that story are mixed together, just as life and art intertwine in unexpected ways.

Adopting the stance of a conventional analytic critic, we might try to describe the relationship of life and art in this poem as a paradox. That would suggest, however, that the apparent conflicts and contradictions between artistic detachment and vividness are somehow resolved into a pattern which will be discerned by a correct reading. I do not see any such resolution in the text, which, for me, leaves open the whole matter, merely inviting me to continue pursuing its enigmas. In that sense, this text is a culmination of the current I have been exploring in post-Civil War poetry. In its highly elaborate way, it takes even further than "Las hilanderas" the question of the interplay between life and art; with its elaborate allusions and shifts of perspective, it illustrates the possibilities of a poetry which invites us to share in its creative play with language and reality.

The picture I have drawn of Spanish poetry after the Civil War is not intended to encompass all of its features, currents or texts. But in tracing the presence and the development of a new attitude toward the poetic text in a number of post-War works and poets, I would like to suggest a change in orientation to the whole period that merits further examination. The movement away from the Symbolist and post-Symbolist notion of the poem as cohesive repository of meaning to a view of the poetic text as creative play of linguistic levels and as stimulus to the creativity of the reader, if true, invites us to revise our past interpretations and methods of study.[26] Taking into account insights offered by deconstructive and reader-response critics, we will re-read poems from this period not with the goal of unearthing their true meanings, but in an effort to take part in their exploration of poetic language, of art, and of reality, and to become more fully attuned to the discoveries made possible by the poetic word.

NOTES

[1]For overviews of earlier post-Civil War poetry, see Félix Grande, *Apuntes sobre poesía española de posguerra* (Madrid: Taurus, 1970), and Victor G. de la Concha, *La poesía española de posguerra: teoría e historia de sus movimientos* (Madrid: Prensa Española, 1973).

[2]Aleixandre, *Algunos caracteres de la nueva poesía española* (Madrid: Instituto de España, 1958) 8.

[3]See Bousoño, "Poesía contemporánea y poesía postcontemporánea" [1961], included in the fourth edition of his *Teoría de la expresión poética* (Madrid: Gredos, 1966) 566-69.

[4]Castellet, *Veinte años de poesía española, 1939-1959* (Barcelona: Seix Barral, 1960) 27ff.

[5]Alonso, *Hijos de la ira; diario íntimo*, 2d. ed. in "Austral" series (Madrid: Espasa-Calpe, 1958) 13.

[6]Silver, "Tradition as Originality in 'Hijos de la ira,'" *Bulletin of Hispanic Studies* 47 (1970): 124-30. For a discussion of the book's background, see Elias Rivers, ed., *Hijos de la ira* (Barcelona: Labor, 1970) 7-22.

[7]For a study of point of view and narrative in *Hijos de la ira*, see my *Dámaso Alonso*, 2nd. ed. (Madrid: Cátedra, 1974), ch. III.

[8]See Stycos, "Intertextuality in the Poetry of Blas de Otero" [unpub.].

I take the term "horizon of expectation" from Hans Robert Jauss, who uses it to discuss the ways in which a reader's knowledge of previous literary works affects his/her responses to a text. See *Toward an Aesthetic of Reception* (Minneapolis: University of Minnesota Press, 1982) 22-32.

[9]On these characteristics of Celaya's work, see Sharon Keefe Ugalde, *Gabriel Celaya* (Boston: Twayne Publishers, 1978) 43-45, 82-91. On 128-29, Ugalde discusses Celaya's poetics. The latter is explained in his *El arte como lenguaje* (Bilbao: Conferencias y Ensayos, 1951).

[10]The shift from a view of the literary work as a static repository of meanings (which dominated not only "New Criticism" but also the whole Symbolist tradition) to the notion of the text as a system of signs, the value of which is open to question, is a fundamental contribution of structuralist and post-structuralist

criticism. On this subject see Roland Barthes, "From Work to Text," in Josué V. Harari, ed., *Textual Strategies* (Ithaca: Cornell University Press, 1979) 73-81. This shift, in my opinion, facilitates the new view of the poem as subject to creative revision and extension on the part of the reader and underlies what I take to be the central characteristics of post-War Spanish poetry.

[11] "Poesía contemporánea y poesía postcontemporánea," *Teoría*, 4th ed., 551-76.

[12] For an overview of this generation see ch. 1 of my *Poetry of Discovery: The Spanish Generation of 1956-1971* (Lexington: University Press of Kentucky, 1982), and José Olivio Jiménez, "Poesía y poética de la joven generación española," *Hispania* 49 (1966): 195-205.

[13] Badosa, "Primero hablemos de Júpiter (La poesía como medio de conocimiento)," *Papeles de Son Armadans* 10.29 (1958): 149-50; Valente, *Las palabras de la tribu* (Madrid: Siglo XXI de España, 1971) 7. I have studied the poetics of this generation of *Poetry of Discovery*, 6-9.

[14] Rodríguez, qtd. in Francisco Ribes, ed., *Poesía última: Selección* (Madrid: Taurus, 1963) 88.

[15] Persin, "José Angel Valente: Poem as Process," *Taller Literario* 1 (1980): 24-41; Debicki, *Poetry of Discovery*, ch. 6; and "Intertextuality and Reader Response in the Poetry of J.A. Valente," *Hispanic Review* 51 (1983): 251-67.

[16] See *Poetry of Discvoery*, 75-77; Miller, "Nonsense Through Intertextuality in the Poetry of A. González" [unpub.]; and Douglas Benson, "Linguistic Parody and Reader Response in the Works of Angel González," *Anales de la Literatura Española Contemporánea* 7 (1982): 11-30.

Benson has also studied perceptively the way in which Francisco Brines invites the reader to collaborate in his poems; see "Memory, Tradition and the Reader in the Poetry of Francisco Brines," *MLN* 99 (1984): 308-26.

[17] Bousoño, "La poesía de C. Rodríguez," Rodríguez, *Poesía 1953-1966* (Madrid: Plaza & Janés, 1971) 7-35; Miller, "Elementos metapoéticos en un poema de C. Rodríguez," *Explicación de Textos Literarios* 8 (1979-80): 127-36; *Poetry of Discovery*, ch. 3.

[18] I take the text from Rodríguez, *Desde mis poemas* (Madrid: Cátedra, 1983) 230.

[19] See my *Poetry of Discovery* 42-46.

[20] Published in Barcelona by Barral Editores.

[21] "La poesía de Guillermo Carnero," in Carnero, *Ensayo de una teoría de la visión (Poesía 1966-1977)* (Madrid: Hiperión, 1979) 11-68.

[22] Gimferrer, "Notas parciales sobre poesía española de posguerra," Salvador Clotas and Gimferrer, *Treinta años de literatura* (Barcelona: Kairos, 1971) 91-108. See also Grande, *Apuntes sobre poesía española de posguerra*.

[23]Timothy Rogers, "Verbal Collage in Pedro Gimferrer's 'Poemas, 1963-1969,'" *Hispania* 67.2 (1984): 207-213.

[24]Bousoño, "La poesía de Guillermo Carnero," 62-67.

[25]Amorós, *Ludia* (Madrid: Adonais, 1983) 62-63. See also Ovid, *Metamorphoses*, trans. Rolfe Humphries (Bloomington: Indiana University Press, 1968) 16-20.

[26]If we accept the attitude of recent deconstructive and reader-response criticism, of course, we would have to say that *all* texts are open, and that the notion of a poem inviting a definitive reading, which I have been linking to the Symbolist tradition, is fundamentally erroneous. I would nevertheless argue that, correct or not, such a notion was underlying the poetics and the goals of pre-Civil War poetry and that it manifests itself in the ways in which typical poems of the time strive for closure. The post-War poetry I have been examining, on the other hand, is built on the premise of an open text and produces significantly different experiences in the extent to which it invites the collaboration of the reader (even though the differences might be a matter of degree). On this issue see Jacques Derrida, *Of Grammatology*, trans. G. Spivak (Baltimore: Johns Hopkins, 1974) 22-24, and J. Hillis Miller, "Stevens' Rock and Criticism as Cure, II," *Georgia Review* 30 (1976): 330-48.

INTERTEXTUALITY IN SELECTED SPANISH POETS SINCE 1939: INTERTEXT/POETICS/READER

Maria Nowakowska Stycos
Cornell University

In recent years, Hispanic poets have shown a new freedom in assimilating other texts into their own. This practice, referred to as *intertextuality* by the critics, presupposes the presence of a text within a text. For example, Angel González's "Poética No. 4" contains an easily identifiable line from Bécquer:

> Poesía eres tú
> dijo un poeta
> – y esa vez era cierto –
> mirando al Diccionario de la Lengua.[1]

"Poesia eres tú," the *intertext,* and the following lines by Angel González, the *exotext,* together form the new *text.* The original or parental work, here Bécquer's *rima,* can be referred to as the *paratext.* This terminology to describe the architecture of an intertextual poem has been suggested by Gustavo Pérez Firmat. Pérez Firmat also proposes that intertextuality as a critical concept should include, in addition to the grafting of one text onto another, "a commonality of conventions, style, or a shared Weltanschauung."[2] Andrew P. Debicki applies the term in this broader sense in his chapter on Gloria Fuertes in *Poetry of Discovery.*[3] In this paper, the use of the term *intertextuality* will be further extended to include a single poetic phrase or word unmistakably associated with another author. The poems discussed here belong to the period of the 1960's and the 1970s when there is a higher incidence of intertextuality – and all share poetics as their common theme. It is the belief of this writer that intertextual relationships can help clarify aspects of meaning not easily accessible otherwise. In addition, since the aesthetic implications of intertextuality are not yet fully understood, the effect of the intertext within individual poems will also be examined as well as its function in the creation of meaning through the intervention of the reader.

"Poética No. 4," as the title suggests, is a quest for a poetics. Because the borrowed line is rather cryptic by itself, in order to understand the message it embodies it is necessary not only to place it in Bécquer's *rima* but also within the broader context of Bécquer's poetic art. The poem's meaning depends on the line's capacity for evoking the reader's recollection of Bécquer's late Romantic poetry and poetics, as it is an assertion of the ineffable quality of poetry. It stands here in stark contrast to a most prosaic, down-to-earth statement on poetry: "dijo el poeta / – y esa vez era cierto – /

mirando al Diccionario de la Lengua." Even so, the words "poet" and "dictionary" serve as a reminder that the poet's tool is language and that his task is to find a poetic language capable of embodying our contemporary reality.

While Bécquer's line inspires a nostalgic look to the past and the new prosaic lines evoke shocked surprise, the poem's meaning derives from the tension of both these inappropriate statements. After the first moment of nostalgia, the reader realizes that Bécquer's language no longer expresses our present-day aesthetics or attitudes. At the same time, while we recognize that language is a science, we reject the notion that the poet's task could be accomplished simply by consulting the dictionary. What then should the new poetic language be? The text itself provides no ready answer but rather a framework or perspective that engages the reader in a consideration of the question.

The intertext serves as a kind of shorthand to bring to bear on the new text the full range of meaning of the paratext, which is not just the single *rima* but Bécquer's poetics in general. The significance of the excised segment does not derive from its length but rather its power of evocation. The poem's message is generated by the reader's ability to recognize and respond to the borrowed line and to create meaning on the interface of the paratext and the exotext: Bécquer's poetics and Angel González's lines. The reader is led to conclude that poetry, while nourished by a superior knowledge of language, must also contain an element of the ineffable, of mystery.[4]

While on a theoretical level it may appear that there is nothing new in this formulation, the context, our present-day materialism, our lack of respect for what cannot be measured or explained scientifically, lend meaning and freshness to this conclusion. In addition, the poet's lucid, unsentimental presentation predisposes the reader to become seriously engaged in the subject. Much of the excitement of this mini-poem comes from the thought process initiated by the text's expressed subject. In the search for a modern poetics, old and new values are tested – a romantic and a pragmatic approach to literature and to the world. Finally, the technique of involving the reader in the creative process, the method of indirection, the terseness and brevity of expression, all contribute to the poem's effectiveness. This very style is a successful model of what is acceptable to a modern reader, contrasting with the more expansive late Romantic style, once cherished perhaps by the very readers González is addressing. Let us also note that the traditional roles of poet and reader are redefined in an intertextual poem. While the reader shares in the creative process, the poet participates as a reader of other texts.

It is significant that intertextuality, with its involvement of the reader in the creative process, occurs frequently at a time when new theories of reading and aesthetic response have underscored the importance of both the reader and texts in the creation of meaning. Julia Kristeva views texts as "mosaics" of other works: "every text takes shape as a mosaic of citations, every text is the absorption and transformation of other texts."[5] Robert Scholes suggests that the reader's knowledge of other literary works animates the "words on the page and transforms them into a poem."[6] Wolfgang Iser writes that: "When a work is produced, the creative act is only an incomplete, abstract impulse; if the author existed all on his own, he could write as much as he liked, but his work would never see the light of day as an object, and he would have to lay down his pen in despair. The process of writing, however, includes a dialectic correlative, the process of reading, and these two independent acts require two differently active people."[7]

Critics have shown that many of the poets of the second post-Civil War generation are highly conscious of the problematics in modern poetics. Francisco Brines and Angel González have thematized the role of the reader in their poems expressing helplessness or despair at the unreliability of language as a means of communication. In "Al lector," Brines suggests that as the act of reading distances the poet from his work, the meaning of words is blurred so that they resemble black stains on the white page of the book rather than linguistic signs carrying a clear message. Ultimately, the reader sees only his own image rather than the poet's.

Crees que me percibes en estas manchas negras del papel
en ese territorio, ya no mío, de la desolación.

Las saqué del vacío,
pude mudarlas por silencio,
y ahora serían ellas el espejo de mí, no de vosotros.[8]

Using surprisingly similar imagery, Angel González suggests in "Poética a la que intento a veces aplicarme" (311) that to write a poem, to try to fix meaning in words, is as an attempt at marking the surface of water. The poet's lack of control over the meaning of language is expressed through imagery suggesting distortion and chance deformation. The reader who tries to make sense of the poem ends by seeing his own reflection, if he sees anything at all.

Escribir un poema: marcar la piel del agua
suavemente, los signos
se deforman, se agrandan
expresan lo que quieren
la brisa, el sol, las nubes,
se distienden, se tensan, hasta
que el hombre que los mira
— adormecido el viento,

la luz alta –
o ve su propio rostro
o – transparencia pura, hondo
fracaso – no ve nada.

As we read the work of such poets as Francisco Brines, Angel
González or José Angel Valente, we discover a constant preoccupa-
tion with the creation of a new poetic language. José Angel Valente
summarizes the contemporary poet's problematic when he writes:
"Perdimos las palabras, el canto y el cantar."9 By resorting to traditional versification, he not only underscores the absence of a poetic
language capable of expressing our reality but also the absence of a
modern poetics. It seems plausible to conclude that in an effort to
communicate, these poets borrow from other texts to build on the
known and therefore predictable signs of meaning. The intertext is a
fixed or stable point of orientation used by the sender in the composition of his message and by the receiver – reader or critic – to
decode it.

A careful analysis of intertextuality could be particularly useful in
a study of poetics. For example, Francisco Brines's "Versos épicos:
Virgilio en Trápani" ends with the phrase "Yo canto la pureza."10
The line is difficult to account for with any degree of precision until
we realize a possible intertextual reference to Juan Ramón Jiménez's
"poesía pura." The poet's own modern diction is contrasted with the
epic tradition of Virgil. The intertextual reference to the Aeneid,
Book V, is created through the title and subtitle and the comparison
of two modern youths to Euryalus and Nisus; and the setting, Sicily,
is common to both. An heroic perspective is contrasted with an anti-
climactic vision of two modern-day lovers who will never match the
heroic deeds of Virgil's characters: they will never build a city and
may even forget each other – their love being temporal and human.
The poet justifies the unembellished style, his lack of elevated tone,
by insisting that it must be adapted to his subject. He refuses to in-
vent the unusual or heroic, preferring his role as an observer of
present-day reality in which he, too, is a participant.11

No imagino un suceso desusado
para cantar con elevado tono, con acento
de llama . . .
es muy baja mi voz.
. . . .
yo canto la pureza.

In this context, "pureza" is affirmed as a positive value and could
be compared to Juan Ramón Jiménez's "naked" rather than "pure"
poetry, as defined by John Wilcox. "In relative terms, a 'naked'
poet's priority will be truth; a 'pure' poet's, beauty."12 Wilcox considers that Juan Ramón's reading of Yeats led him in the direction of

"naked" poetry, while the French Symbolists, Mallarmé and Valéry lead toward the "pure" aesthetic. Citing a 1943 letter to Luis Cernuda in which the words "sencillo" and "natural" are used, Wilcox argues that "after the poet's move to the New World, the 'natural,' 'naked' and 'open' impulses appear and compete more forcefully for expression ..." (518). In Wilcox's view, the "pure" poem is "the norm after the time Jiménez left Moguer to settle in Madrid (1912)" (518). Surprisingly, perhaps, the polarities and conflicts which underlie Juan Ramón's poetry appear to be relevant considerations for the poets of the second post-Civil War generation. In another poem, "Invitación a un blanco mantel," Brines buries an intertextual reference to "Intelijencia" (the italics in the following poem are mine).

> Blanco mantel.
> Es un error; pues no hay color, ni hay lugar prevenido, ni
>   nada que soporte
> la que habrá de ser luz, o lo indeciso.
>
> . . . .
> Ya puedes, no invitado,
> presentarte en el hueco,
> y puesto que careces de movimiento real, y aun del furtivo,
> estás en condiciones de injuriar el mantel,
> y si lo manchas (pues no hay color, ni hay lugar prevenido,
>   ni nada que soporte
> la opción de lo indeciso, engaño o luz)
> *ya puedes conocerte. Date un nombre.*[13]

The image of the white tablecloth suggests the writing and the reading process. (We cannot rule out a possible internal intertextual relationship with "Al lector.") The whiteness of the page is evoked by the whiteness of the tablecloth, which also suggests a celebration, a dinner shared with friends. Through a series of propositions no sooner made than denied, the poet expresses the frustrations posed by the ambiguities of language and reading. Iser considers the reading process as complementary to writing – a positive force. Not so Brines. In "Invitación a un blanco mantel," published in 1977, eleven years after "Al lector," Brines's skepticism toward writing and communication reaches the verge of despair. The poem's ending, "Date un nombre," is an ironic allusion to Juan Ramón's "el nombre exacto de las cosas" in "Intelijencia."[14] In order to express the rift between the poet and his words and to portray the despair of a poet threatened by silence, Brines resorts to a familiar landmark. It is precisely the contrast with Juan Ramón's hope that the poetic process will reveal the identity of things by naming them that punctuates Brines's pessimism and conveys it to his readers.

In "Orden. (Poética a la que otros se aplican.)," Angel González also chooses Juan Ramón's "Intelijencia" as his point of orientation:

"Sé puro; / no nombres; no ilumines" (312). José Angel Valente, in "Noviembre" (253), creates a parody of Juan Ramón's "Noche de todos los santos." Gloria Fuertes states quite simply in "Ya no destrozo la poesía": "me gusta más la violada realidad / que la santísima pureza juanramoniana."[15] Gloria Fuertes is clearly alluding to Juan Ramón Jiménez as a "pure" poet, more dedicated to beauty than to truth. Wilcox observes that although "the concept of 'poesía desnuda' did preoccupy Juan Ramón from around 1915 to 1920 . . . In the case of the naked female body, as 'Vino, primero" testifies, this amounts to focusing not on its immediate sensual beauty, but on its symbolic interpretation" (513). Another telling intertextual echo of Juan Ramón is to be found in Fuertes's "A un artista" (326):

> Prefiero la selva al Museo
> prefiero un muchacho vivo
> a un cuadro muerto
>
> Prefiero
> ver al hombre
> no a su libro impreso . . .
> ¡No me contéis el crimen,
> prefiero ver al preso!

The phrase "un muchacho vivo / . . . a un cuadro muerto" is a transposition of a title of a poem by Jiménez, "A un niño muerto en un cuadro," published in *Estío* in 1916.[16] Gloria Fuertes here affirms her passionate interest in life or "truth" even when it is "impure," sensuous or less than perfect. Her message is strengthened by the intertextual allusion to an early poem by Juan Ramón Jiménez.

These intertextual connections are signs that lead to a more complete understanding both of the individual poems in which they appear and of the aesthetic framework within which these poets write. Juan Ramón Jiménez's poetics, whether rejected or modified, emerges as the common *paratext* of the four poets quoted. They reject "purity" when beauty rather than "truth" would become the primary concern of poetry. We can speculate that this generation of poets, while turning away from the "social" poetry of the first post-Civil War generation, has retained a strong commitment to the expression and definition of man as situated in time and place.[17] In their concern with form and lack of adornment, they turn toward the poetics of Juan Ramón Jiménez, even if they sometimes reject or modify it. Juan Ramón as their common *paratext* creates a *de facto* bond between the members of the group — an aspect of intertextuality yet to be developed and tested as a critical consideration.

The scope of intertextuality as a source for poetic creation or its potential as a critical tool has not yet been fully defined. In *Ríos caudales; apología del 27*, Concha Zardoya has more recently expanded the intertextual sources on which the poet draws for meaning.[18] To understand these poems, the reader must be familiar not only with the work of the poets of 1927 but also with the relevant literary criticism. A poet who is also a teacher and critic – like so many Spanish poets of this century –, Zardoya is well aware of the influence of texts read on our consciousness and our capacity for understanding and communication. Perhaps this is the first time in history that authors can count on significant numbers of readers who are as well read in poetry as in literary criticism. Without that, intertextuality would lead to hermeticism rather than communication.

NOTES

[1]Angel González, *Palabra sobre palabra*, 2nd ed. (Barcelona: Barral Editores, 1977). All quotations are from this edition. Earlier editions were published by Seix Barral (1968) and Poesía Para Todos (1965).

[2]Gustavo Pérez Firmat, "Apuntes para un modelo de la intertextualidad en literatura," *Romanic Review* 69 (1978): 1-14.

[3]Andrew P. Debicki, *Poetry of Discovery: The Spanish Generation of 1956-1971* (Lexington: The University of Kentucky Press, 1982) 81-101. See also the discussion of "Poética No. 4" in the chapter on Angel González, 79.

[4]Angel González thematizes the ineffability of poetry in other poems, for example, "Ahí, donde fracasan las palabras," or "Oda a la noche o letra para tango."

[5]Julia Kristeva, *Semiotikè: Recherches pour une sémanalyse* (Paris: Seuil, 1969) 146. I follow Jonathan Culler's translation in *Structuralist Poetics* (Ithaca: Cornell University Press, 1975) 139.

[6]Robert Scholes, *Semiotics and Interpretation* (New Haven and London: Yale University Press, 1982) 38.

[7]Wolfgang Iser, *The Act of Reading: A Theory of Aesthetic Response* (Baltimore and London: The Johns Hopkins University Press, 1987) 108.

[8]Francisco Brines, *Insistencias en Luzbel* (Madrid: Visor, 1977).

[9]José Angel Valente, *Punto Cero* (Barcelona: Barral Editores, 1972). The poem "Perdimos las palabras" actually belongs to *Breve son (1953-1968)*, first published by El Bardo in 1968. See also Margaret H. Persin's "José Angel Valente: Poem as Process," *Taller Literario* 1, no. 1 (1980): 24-41 for an intertextual connection between Valente's "La rosa necesaria" and Juan Ramón Jiménez.

[10]Francisco Brines, *Palabras a la oscuridad* (Madrid: Insula, 1966).

[11]I am following my own analysis of the poem presented in a paper at a special session at the MLA convention in 1979, "Metapoetry and the Spanish Post-Civil War Poets." The paper was titled: "The Poetics of Francisco Brines, or Brines on Brines."

53

[12]John Wilcox, "'Naked' versus 'Pure' Poetry in Juan Ramón Jiménez, with Remarks on the Impact of W.B. Yeats," *Hispania* 66 (1983): 511-21. All quotations by Wilcox are from this article.

[13]Francisco Brines, *Insistencias en Luzbel.*

[14]Juan Ramón Jiménez, *Segunda antología poética (1898-1918)* (Madrid: Espasa-Calpe, S.A., 1976).

[15]Gloria Fuertes, *Obras incompletas* (Madrid: Ediciones Cátedra, 1977). Andrew P. Debicki includes Fuertes in *Poetry of Discovery* in the same generation as Brines, Valente and González.

[16]Juan Ramón Jiménez, *Libros de poesía*, 3rd ed. (Madrid: Aguilar, 1967). I owe this find to John Wilcox.

[17]See, for example, José Olivio Jiménez, *Diez años de poesía española: (1960-1970)* (Madrid: Insula, 1971): "Haciéndose casi portavoz de su generación, Claudio Rodríguez definirá la poesía como el intento de 'exponer el destino humano en relación de totalidad con la época en que se produce y con el hombre que la escribe . . .'" (21).

[18]Concha Zardoya, *Ríos caudales: apología del 27* (Madrid: Corcel, 1982).

POSTURAS DEL POETA ANTE SU PALABRA EN LA ESPAÑA DE POSGUERRA

Douglass Rogers
University of Texas at Austin

Nos proponemos examinar algunas señales de lo que podría llamarse la desmitificación de la palabra en la poesía española de posguerra. A modo de revisión parcial de clasificaciones que inevitablemente resultaron algo simplistas, volveremos de nuevo sobre algunas facetas de una aparente polaridad estética, identificada principalmente con una poesía esteticista frente a una realista, visión impuesta por el período histórico, como es bien sabido. Intentaremos destacar ejemplos de variaciones y tendencias contrarias a la clasificación, y al llegar a la década de los sesenta, señalaremos una mutación en el carácter del mismo fenómeno estudiado. Las muestras comentadas aquí provienen casi exclusivamente de una selección de alusiones explícitas hechas por los poetas a su palabra dentro de su obra creativa. Por lo tanto nuestra investigación sólo aspira a sugerir o confirmar ciertas direcciones y patrones importantes, y no pretende esbozar un cuadro completo.

Se ha ido descubriendo cada vez más que las manifestaciones metapoéticas de tiempos modernos ofrecen un valioso complemento para la crítica. Con frecuencia revelan aspectos de la creación no encontrados en encuestas, prólogos o ensayos, como si sorprendiéramos a un poeta hablando para sí, libre de presiones públicas o cuestiones ajenas a su arte. Aunque nunca ha sido la regla que fuera el poeta el mejor crítico de su propia obra, cabe recordar una observación de Gerardo Diego: «Ni tampoco otro que no sea el artista mismo conoce a ciencia cierta las intenciones generales de su arte ni las particulares de cada ensayo concreto de obra».[1] ¿Quién sino Francisco Brines mismo pudo decirnos: «No tuve amor a las palabras», en *Insistencias en Luzbel*?[2] Cuando el poeta habla de «mi palabra», de «las palabras», del acto de nombrar, o usa términos de semejante índole, ello puede interpretarse normalmente como forma metonímica de aludir al lenguaje, a la expresión, o hasta a la poesía. A pesar de lo arriesgado que es aislar fragmentos, un estudio de estas manifestaciones puede aportar una nueva perspectiva a nuestro conocimiento de la actitud de un poeta, o de un grupo de poetas, frente a su medio artístico.

Referencias a «la palabra» se han hecho cada vez más frecuentes en la obra de poetas de la época posterior a la Guerra Civil, pero es posible ver la práctica como una veta de la metapoesía que se remonta hasta la segunda década del siglo, cuando se da a conocer la fascinación de Juan Ramón Jiménez por los nombres, sobre todo «el nombre exacto de las cosas», fascinación perpetuada en Salinas y

Guillén. En ellos se reflejaba una concepción de la palabra como algo dotado de poder mágico, capaz de transformaciones extraordinarias. El entusiasmo del poeta «nombrador» ante su palabra justa es muy semejante al del creacionista o ultraísta ante el poder de la metáfora, pero la aparente contradicción es sólo ilusoria, puesto que «nombre exacto» y metáfora no son de veras polos opuestos: la metáfora puede ser un modo de nombrar y la nominación puede tener una dimensión metafórica, cuestión en que no nos toca entrar aquí. Howard Young ha señalado cómo en el Juan Ramón nombrador se inaugura un nuevo estilo, un nuevo modo de concebir la poesía, inspirado en gran parte por los *Imagists* ingleses y norteamericanos, tanto por su *Credo* como por su obra.[3] Pero Young demuestra también cómo Juan Ramón lo hace sin perder por completo su herencia simbolista, notablemente, la fe en el poder del verbo, preocupación identificada sobre todo con Mallarmé. Hugo Friedrich encuentra las raíces de esta posición simbolista frente a la palabra ya en Novalis, cuyos términos son reveladores:

> Novalis toma de la magia el concepto de conjuro. «Toda palabra es un conjuro», es un modo de provocar y subyugar las cosas que nombra. De aquí el «hechizo de la fantasía» y la afirmación: «el mago es poeta», y vice-versa.[4]

Algo de este espíritu perdura en el Juan Ramón de «¡Intelijencia, dame ...», a pesar del nuevo rigor y la ausencia total de sentimentalismo. Se trata de un acto místico para el poeta, un incantatio que aspira a invocar una palabra todopoderosa, más allá del lenguaje ordinario, y por lo tanto no encontrada, comparable en esto con la «cifra» buscada por Bécquer.[5]

La concepción del nombre poético como algo trascendental e inexplicable sigue viva en Salinas. En *Todo más claro*, donde se describe el nacimiento del verbo poético, de aquellas «huestes calladas» o «santas palabras»,[6] la estructuración de una experiencia mística, con recuerdos específicos de San Juan de la Cruz, es ya menos discutible de lo que era en Juan Ramón. El proceso inefable requiere términos extraordinarios:

> Un algo que inicia ya,
> muy misterioso, el trabajo
> de coger su flor al mundo
> – alquimia, birlibirloque –
> para siempre, y sin tocarlo. (660)

Por fin, dice el poeta: «en el papel amanece / una palabra», luego, de la nueva luz producida por el poema: «¡qué sencillo el gran milagro!» (666, 667). De nuevo en el ensayo, originalmente discurso, «Aprecio y defensa del lenguaje», Salinas habla del «Poder de la palabra» y de las «Maravillas de la lengua».[7] Afirma reconocer en el lenguaje una «misión primordial comunicativa», para luego preguntar: «Pero no es, antes algo más que eso?» (21). Luego se lanza a una inspirada descripción de dos casos que podríamos llamar de «nominación primordial», en boca de un niño que descubre por primera vez una flor, y de una niña (según el poeta, hija de Juan Maragall) que «pronuncia como un conjuro» la palabra «mar», al ver por primera vez el Mediterráneo (21-23). Queda claramente sugerida aquí la idea de la palabra como instrumento mitificante del hombre primitivo, quien con su descubrimiento verbal crea, o re-crea y organiza su mundo.[8]

De Jorge Guillén nos limitaremos a mencionar aquí sólo el familiar poema «Los nombres», donde el verbo aparece dotado de eternidad: «Pero quedan los nombres», recordándonos un poema de Juan Ramón de 1911, «Creemos los nombres», que acaba con los versos: «Del amor y las rosas, / no ha de quedar sino los nombres».[9]

Juan Ramón, Salinas, y Guillén, tres poetas de máximo rigor y lucidez, tres agudas mentes críticas, todos exentos de rezagados excesos románticos, al invocar la palabra poética, lo hacen en términos mitificantes. Hasta aquí parece confirmada la primera parte de la división que hizo José María Castellet de la poesía española del siglo veinte en dos tipos fundamentales (en la introducción a su controversial antología y estudio de 1960): tres décadas de simbolismo, seguidas por la poesía realista que surge en los años treinta, para culminar después de la Guerra Civil.[10] Al poeta «de tradición simbolista» lo caracteriza como «un ser privilegiado, un solitario, un iluminado, un encantador de palabras, un artista mágico».[11]

¿Cuándo se nota una reacción? La «Poética» de Vicente Aleixandre en la segunda edición de la *Antología* de Gerardo Diego, de 1934, parece comprobar ya la existencia de un diálogo antagónico, aunque no sea un ataque precisamente contra los poetas mencionados hasta aquí. Dice Aleixandre:

Frente a la divinización de la palabra, frente a esa casi obscena delectación de la *maestría* o dominio verbal del artífice que trabaja la talla, confundiendo el estello del vidrio que tiene entre sus manos con la profunda luz creadora, hay que afirmar, hay que exclamar con verdad: No, la poesía no es *cuestión de palabras.*[12]

Unos veinte años después, confirmada ya su nueva dirección, el mismo poeta diría en el poema «Sin nombre»: «No, no quedan los nombres».[13] Aunque se trata aquí de nombres propios que no existen para los seres marginados, humildes anónimos, es difícil que no se haya interpretado como parte de la reacción «realista», tan marcada en Aleixandre. «¿Vivir en ellas?» pregunta en «Las palabras del poeta» (1968), «Las palabras mueren. / Bellas son al sonar, mas nunca duran».[14]

57

En las primeras dos décadas después de 1939, la práctica entre los nuevos poetas de reflexionar sobre la palabra poética, dentro de su obra, no sólo no disminuye sino que experimenta un incremento, fenómeno que podría parecer paradójico, dada la constancia de la rebelión contra la poesía narcisista, identificada tanto con el Garcilasismo como con ciertas modas de preguerra. Sin embargo, tales manifestaciones en general son parte íntegra del sentido de crisis que impone al poeta una revisión de todas las facetas de la expresión poética.[15] El aspecto más familiar de esta revisión tal vez sea la programática, bien delineada por Castellet, quien hace resaltar la polaridad entre dos tipos de lenguaje poético:

> Por último, mientras que el lenguaje de la poesía de tradición simbolista no sólo no pretende ser comunicativo, significativo o lógico, sino que, por el contrario, busca alcanzar al lector a través de la musicalidad y la sugestión sensual de las palabras, el lenguaje del poeta de actitud realista tiende, inexcusablemente, a restituir a la palabra la función comunicativa de un significado inmediato y real: se pasa así de una poesía esotérica y enigmática, a una poesía de clara significación humana, escrita en un lenguaje coloquial y llano.[16]

Teniendo en cuenta esta cita como trasfondo, preferimos dejar de lado temas refamiliares, como la poesía social, la poesía como comunicación o como arma, para ver otros problemas más bien estéticos que históricos, que se manifiestan en la obra de poetas individuales, solos frente a su palabra. Entre ellos uno duradero y fundamental es el de la vulgarización del lenguaje poético, no tanto en el sentido anti-purista de Neruda, sino en el de la aspiración a volver a una lengua viva que se mantenga fiel al habla del pueblo. En sí esto no representa novedad: Wordsworth, Bécquer, T.S. Eliot, Antonio Machado y otros han defendido el principio, cada uno a su propia manera.

Hasta sin entrar en la problemática de la poesía social, podemos identificar señales de un genuino amor por la lengua identificada con el pueblo. Nuria Pares, en un poema titulado «Palabras . . .», habla con cariño de lo que ella llama «esas viejas palabras de la tierra»:

> Suenan en mis oídos, me acompañan,
> dialogan entre ellas como el lento
> y despacioso doblar de las campanas
> de la iglesia mayor y el tintineo
> humilde de una esquila.[17]

En 1957 José Hierro dijo (en el prólogo a *Poesía del momento*): «Mi lengua pretende ser lengua de la calle, la que hablo con los que convivo. Palabras viejas, cargadas de sentido, que bastan al cordial entendedor».[18] Este deseo de conservar en su obra la vitalidad del lenguaje familiar podría verse como polo opuesto del procedimiento de selección de vocablos que él encontraba en Guillén, cuyo resultado le parecía un lenguaje enrarecido y frío:

En el vocabulario guilleniano, tan cuidado, son frecuentes las palabras que, aun designando sensaciones, hablan exclusivamente al cerebro. Desprecia toda palabra que se acerque al lenguaje vulgar. [...] Dirá júbilo, y no alegría. Dirá cándido, y no blanco, siempre que sea posible. Y palabras como disidencia, equilibrio, concluye, sobrehumana, clarividente, azar, rectora, no son extrañas, ni mucho menos en sus poemas.[19]

Sin embargo, quien conoce la obra de Hierro habrá podido ver dentro de ella la afición por la pintura, por la música, y por la palabra en cuanto medio artístico. Si en el conocido poema «Para un esteta», pudo decir: «Tú que hueles la flor de la bella palabra / acaso no comprendas las mías sin aroma», él mismo parece desdecirse unos versos más adelante al afirmar: «Y lo demás, palabras, palabras y palabras, / ¡ay, palabras maravillosas!»[20] Además, para complementar, o corregir, cualquier «credo», siempre conviene tener en cuenta la obra creativa: como ha visto David Bary, éste es uno de los verdaderos poetas nombradores de su generación.[21] En el poema que encabezaba *Cuanto sé de mí*, «Nombrar perecedero», se encuentra una negación del valor eterno o eternizante de la palabra:

No tengo miedo nombraros.
Qué importa que no le importen
al que viva, cuando yo
haya muerto, vuestros nombres.[22]

Pero a pesar de ello, este poema demuestra hasta qué punto la palabra no ha perdido su misterio para Hierro. Por cierto, es un poema menos juanramoniano que machadiano, un evocativo «nombrar perecedero», que constituye un modo de luchar contra el tiempo, un lirismo fundamentalmente romántico-tradicional:

No tengo miedo nombraros
ya con vuestros nombres,
cosas vivas, transitorias.
. . . .
Vosotras sois lo que sois
para mí: mágico bosque
perecedero, campanas
que regaláis vuestros sones
sólo al que os golpea. Cómo
darlos al que no os oye,
. . . .

59

Mías sois, cosas fugaces,
bajo marchitables nombres.
. . . .
Nombraros ¿no es poseeros
para siempre, cosas, nombres?[23]

El proceso bergsoniano en Antonio Machado, con sus «cosas
del ayer, que sois el alma»,[24] llega a veces a extremos proustianos,
es decir, a una convergencia de sensaciones que produce el efecto
de una aprehensión de vida pasada, fenómeno inexplicable, irracio-
nal, y no reproducible sólo por un acto de volición. Y a este Machado
soñador se le aproximaba a veces el Hierro alucinado, de modo que
en la práctica no ha desaparecido el conjuro verbal, aun entre los
que rechazaban «la bella palabra».

Si los poetas más conocidos de la primera generación de posguerra intentaron derrumbar la retórica gastada de otros grupos y
períodos, no por eso pudieron evitar una retórica propia. Y el hastío
con ésta provoca a su turno otra reacción (aunque no se trate de nin-
guna nítida cadena cronológica), pero sin rechazar el lenguaje llano,
que sigue usado y defendido, relacionado en alguna medida con un
desdén por la hipocresía, por la retórica y por cualquier clase de artificio. No obstante, el sabor de la expresión es ya otro, pues los
móviles han cambiado: ya no se trata de una necesidad de purga-
ción del alegado esteticismo o evasionismo, y los poetas ya no acu-
den a recetas programáticas. De los factores que entran en juego,
nos limitaremos aquí a comentar sólo dos: una nueva sofisticación
lingüística y la depresión irónica de la palabra.

Evidencia del primero se vislumbra con creciente frecuencia,
culminando posiblemente en *Ser de palabra* (1978), de José María
Valverde, donde el poeta discurre largamente (y no sin ironía) sobre
una transformación del papel de la lengua en las culturas humanas:

Pero cuando lo comprendí
era mayor, hombre de libros,
y acaso fue porque en alguno
leí la gran perogrullada:
que no hay más mente que el lenguaje,
y pensamos sólo al hablar,
y no queda más mundo vivo
tras las tierras de la palabra.[25]

Aquí la lengua es concebida como sistema de percibir, conocer y
controlar el mundo, o como insinúa el poeta, hasta de serlo. Con las
crecidas dosis de intelectualismo y erudición que van penetrando en
la obra de los poetas de la segunda o tercera generación de posguerra, han podido entrar temas plenamente «lingüísticos».

La obrita de Angel González, «Luz llamada día trece», ¿no puede leerse como ilustración paródica del principio saussuriano de la arbitrariedad del signo?»

> A cada cosa por su solo nombre.
> Pan significa pan; amor, espanto;
> madera, eso; primavera, llanto:
> el cielo, nada; la verdad, el hombre.[26]

Consistente con el realismo de este poeta, sin embargo, el poema contiene una negación del principio que aparece en el poema de Valverde, de que la realidad humana sea una creación mítica, un sistema verbal que reemplace lo que antes se veía erróneamente como realidad externa independiente:

> .... ¡Cuánto
> más verdadera que cualquier pronombre
>
> es esa luz que cuaja el aire en día!
> Hoy es la luz llamada día trece
> de materia de mayo y sol, digamos.

En «La palabra», de *Palabra sobre palabra*, el lector encuentra una nueva versión – mejor dicho, inversión – del mito del nacimiento de la palabara en una época paradisíaca. Siguiendo un patrón de detallada reconstrucción histórica, familiar a sus lectores, el poeta por fin nos lleva al descubrimiento:

> Igual que un pájaro
> salta desde una rama,
> de ese modo
> surgió en el aire limpio de aquel día
> la palabra:
>   *amor*.[27]

No se debe concluir por nuestras citas que Angel González sea de los poetas más inclinados a pensar en términos lingüísticos formales, pero muestras de este tipo valen como indicio de que entre los poetas de este período ha habido un aumento de tales conocimientos. Es de esperar que éstos aporten un nuevo grado de sobriedad a la lengua, y que la sólida base científica de la lingüística contemporánea efectúe cierto desmoronamiento de la tradición de reverencia ante la inefabilidad de la palabra poética. Se trata de una desmitificación menos propagandística o utilitaria que la anterior, más ilustrada y libre de interferencias. Ejemplo de un probable efecto es la debilitación de la idea de dos lenguas, una poética y extraordinaria, y otra utilitaria y ordinaria. Al comentar esta falacia, Emilio Alarcos Llorach ha puesto como ejemplo de «lenguaje ordinario»: «Dame la llave», palabras que, al ser emitidas en una circunstancia específica dependen de contingencias inmediatas y carecen de poesía, mientras que incorporadas a otro sistema, pueden constituir un discurso poético, por ejemplo: «Dame la llave. El mundo es muy oscuro / una puerta ha de haber. Yo no la encuentro».[28]

Si en Angel González se halla también el supremo ejemplo del impacto de la ironía en la expresión poética, conviene primero recordar su actitud ante la lengua poética, una claramente articulada por él y que lo coloca en el mismo bando que José Hierro:

Y cuando hablo de realidad me estoy refiriendo también a la realidad de la materia de la que el poema está hecho: la lengua, el idioma hablado, vivo, que nunca he tratado de destruir (manía obsesiva de algunos colegas), sino de utilizar – cuando no de imitar.[29]

Pero en el tono de la obra de Angel González se respira más que un amor por el habla del pueblo: hay una técnica ironizante plenamente consciente, cuyo carácter denso y polifacético ya ha sido analizado.[30] Nos limitaremos aquí a examinar la estrategia irónica de un solo poema, uno que se encuentra ya en *Aspero-mundo*, y que casi podría leerse como parodia de la exhortación de Juan Ramón, «Intelijencia dame / el nombre exacto de las cosas»: «Me falta una palabra, una palabra / sólo».[31] Ahora la «cifra» buscada por Bécquer, que había de encerrar el «himno gigante», queda reducida a un ingrediente menor, «una sencilla / palabra que haga juego / con . . .», tentativa frustrada del poeta de encontrar *le mot juste*, debido a una serie de distracciones. Contrastemos este fracaso con el final de «Objeto del poema», de José Angel Valente, donde se describe el éxtasis del hallazgo espontáneo:

Yaces
y te comparto, hasta que
un día simple irrumpes
con atributos
de claridad, desde tu misma
manantial excelencia.[32]

A diferencia de este feliz momento lírico, la frase inicial del poema de Angel González, «Me falta una palabra, una palabra / sólo», asalta al oído del lector con todo el prosaísmo de «Dame la llave», de nuestra cita anterior. Aquí la ironía depende del abrupto contraste de lo dicho en el primer verso con una norma sobre el género poético llevada por el lector al poema. En este caso hay un choque con el léxico y la temática consagrados. «Me falta una palabra» podría ser una exclamación, proferida o pensada, sobre la molesta labor de revisión anterior al comienzo formal del poema, como palabras inoportunas escapadas en un teatro al abrirse el telón prematuramente. Pero el poema se compone por el lector en el acto de leer, y en la recreación éste descrubre que ese tono es en efecto el del poema, y esa ironía es el sabor que le presta unidad.

A pesar del carácter penetrante, a veces demoledor, de la ironía en Angel González, como en el caso de Hierro, también hay momentos en que irrumpe el lírico en su propia palabra, asombrándose ante el milagro de la creación poética en términos que son fundamentalmente los de *Todo más claro*, de Salinas:

> Escribir un poema: marcar la piel del agua.
> Suavemente, los signos
> se deforman, se agrandan,
> expresan lo que quieren
> la brisa, el sol, las nubes
> se distienden, se tensan, hasta
> que el hombre que los mira
> − adormecido el viento,
> la luz alta −
> o ve su propio rostro
> o − transparencia pura, hondo
> fracaso − no ve nada.[33]

Hay que confesar que no falta ironía ni en este poema (su título: «Poética. A la que intento a veces aplicarme»), pero a nuestro modo de ver, en este caso el lirismo y la ironía no van fundidos, ni «contaminándose», sino que a pesar de su carácter antitético, coexisten, alternándose, intactos.

En resumen, durante las primeras tres décadas después de la Guerra Civil, se da un notable aumento de momentos en que el poeta se ocupa de su propio medio expresivo, dentro de su obra, probable síntoma de un sostenido esfuerzo de renovación de la lengua poética que caracteriza la época. La variedad de direcciones representadas incluye la preferencia por un lenguaje próximo al habla popular en algunos casos, responde a una agudizada conciencia lingüística en otros, y refleja una visión o técnica ironizante en otros. Prácticamente todas coinciden en representar una oposición a la deificación del verbo poético, postura que ya no le sirve al poeta, a pesar de lo cual surgen con insistencia señales de que sigue en pie una fe en la inexplicable fuerza creativa de la palabra.

NOTES

[1]Gerardo Diego, *Primera antología de sus versos*, 3ª ed. (Buenos Aires: Espasa Calpe, 1944) 13.

[2](Madrid: Visor, 1977) 83.

[3]«The Exact Names,» *Modern Language Notes* 96 (1981): 212-23.

[4]*Estructura de la lírica moderna* (Barcelona: Seix Barral, 1959) 36.

[5]En la rima «Yo sé un himno gigante y extraño»: «Pero en vano es luchar; que no hay cifra / capaz de encerrarlo». *Obras completas* (Madrid: Aguilar, 1964) 435.

[6]Pedro Salinas, *Poesías completas* 2ª ed. (Barcelona: Barral, 1975) 663. Referencias futuras estarán incorporadas al texto. Aunque los poemas de *Todo mas claro* datan de 1937 a 1947, no por eso dejan de ser representativos del Salinas de la época anterior a la Guerra.

[7]Pedro Salinas, *La responsabilidad del escritor* (Barcelona: Seix Barral, 1961): 16 y 19. Otras referencias en el texto.

[8]La semejanza con un texto de Emile Staiger aquí es muy digno de notar: siguiendo un patrón elaborado por Cassirer, Staiger también había aprovechado la imagen del niño para caracterizar lo que llama el «grito emotivo» del «ser lírico». V. *Conceptos fundamentales de poética* (Madrid: Rialp, 1969) 213.

[9]Juan Ramón Jiménez, *Tercera antolojía poética* (Madrid: Biblioteca Nueva, 1975) 254.

[10]José María Castellet, *Veinte años de poesía española (1939-1959)* (Barcelona: Seix Barral, 1960).

[11]Castellet 34.

[12]*Poesía española contemporánea* (Madrid: Taurus, 1959) 494 (2ª ed.: Signo, 1934).

[13]Cit. en Joaquín González Muela y Juan Manuel Rozas, eds., *La generación poética de 1927* (Madrid: Alcalá, 1974) 214.

[14]Muela y Rozas 216.

[15]Lo que sí sorprende fue que la tendencia pasara casi inadvertida por la crítica, con una importante excepción, el largo estudio de David Bary, «Sobre el nombrar poético en la poesía española contemporánea», *Papeles de Son Armadans* 44 (1967): 161-89. La dirección seguida por él difiere bastante de la nuestra, pero Bary muestra bien el carácter múltiple y ambiguo del fenómeno del «nombrar poético».

[16]Castellet 35.

[17]Cit. en José Luis Cano, *Antología de la nueva poesía española*, 4ª ed. (Madrid: Gredos, 1978) 357.

[18]José Hierro, *Poesía del momento* (Madrid: Afrodisio Aguado, 1957) 12.

[19]De papeles privados prestados por el poeta, ca. 1960.

[20]*Poesías completas (1944-1962)* (Madrid: Giner, 1962) 294.

[21]Bary (v. nuestra nota 15).

[22]Hierro, *Poesías completas* 441.

[23]Hierro, *Poesías completas* 441-42.

24Antonio Machado, *Obras, poesía y prosa* (Buenos Aires: Losada, 1964) 110.

25José María Valverde, *Ser de palabra* (Barcelona: Ocnos, 1976) 30.

26Angel González, *Palabra sobre palabra* (Barcelona: Barral, 1972) 93.

27González 172.

28Emilio Alarcos Llorach, «Poesía y estratos de la lengua», *Ensayos y estudios literarios* (Madrid: Jucar, 1976) 248.

29Angel González, *Poemas* (Madrid: Cátedra, 1980) 16.

30Sobre todo en los recientes estudios de Douglas K. Benson: «La ironía, la función del hablante y la experiencia del lector en la poesía de Angel González», *Hispania* 64 (1981): 570-81; «Angel González y *Muestra* (1977): las perspectivas múltiples de una sensibilidad irónica», *RHM* 40 (1978-1979): 42-59.

31González, *Palabra sobre palabra* 19.

32José Angel Valente, *Noventa y nueve poemas* (Madrid: Alianza, 1981) 54.

33Angel González, *Muestra* (Madrid: Turner, 1977) 37.

DIFFÉRANCE
IN THE EARLY POETRY OF ANGEL GONZÁLEZ

Margaret H. Persin
Rutgers University

Critics most often have classified the poetry of Angel González under the headings of social poetry, committed poetry, or poetry of protest.[1] The studies reflecting these judgments concentrate on González's philosophical orientation, world view, or testimonial posture. But this classification is too narrow and simplistic, since it fails to recognize both the thematic diversity and literary creativity that have developed in González's texts between the publication of this first book of verse, *Aspero mundo* (1956), and his latest collection, *Prosemas o menos* (1983). As both Douglas Benson and José Olivio Jiménez have noted, the poetry of Angel González and that of the entire second generation of post-Civil War poets react against the limiting and stultifying tendencies which defined and characterized the earlier post-Civil War generation, namely, thematic dogmatism, monotony of style and expression, impoverished language, and lack of imagination and experimentation.[2]

Most studies of González's poetry focus on his themes and mention only in passing the specific features of his artistic language. But this perspective fails to account for the poet's high level of artistic experimentation and the concomitant participation of the reader in the creative process that results with such experimentation. It is precisely through such devices as multiple speakers, apostrophe, and contrary-to-fact statements that González is able to communicate a wide variety of themes. Therefore, in this study I wish to bring to light some of the aesthetic techniques that the poet utilizes in the construction of his verse. These techniques, I believe, distinguish this poet as a careful, self-conscious and creative stylist, one who uses direct and ordinary language in an extraordinary fashion in order to create unique literary experiences for his readers. Like the other members of his literary generation, González elicits the participation of the reader. For him poetry is not a final result, nor a finished product, but rather a way of knowing the reality which surrounds us all. Through the collaboration of poet, reader, and word the poetic form acquires its meaning. Just as the poem indicates the poet's response to one particular set of circumstances at a particulate moment in time, so each reader brings a unique set of circumstances to the reading of the poet's texts. Meaning evolves with each reader and reading of the texts.[3]

A unifying feature which informs all of Angel González's poetry can best be described by the dialectical relationship of presence versus absence. According to Jonathan Culler, "for presence to function as it is said to, it must have the qualities that supposedly belong to its opposite, absence. Thus, instead of defining absence in terms of presence, as *its* negation, we can treat 'presence' as the effect of a generalized absence or .. of *différance.*"[4] This dialectic of presence and absence, of course, points to the deconstructivist attack on logocentrism and its contention that language itself must accept partial complicity in its failure to communicate unadulterated truth through its structures. A certain linguistic structure can signify one thing, but it can also be coaxed to mean quite the opposite. González takes full advantage of this seeming paradox in order to infuse his texts with undercurrents, resonances and flashes of significance. This double functioning of language to communicate both an explicit and an implicit message necessarily requires the reader's collaboration. Supposedly, a text is complete in and of itself; otherwise, the poet would not have offered it to the public. But González demands that his reader provide a supplement to the proffered text. Culler defines supplement as "an inessential extra, added to something complete in itself, but the supplement is added in order to complete, to compensate for a lack in what was supposed to be complete in itself."[5] The paradoxical cast of language is inescapable: it does and does not communicate, and is and is not complete. It is only through the mediation of the reader that the supposedly impossible gap is bridged.[6]

The dialectic of presence and absence is manifested in various ways on the suprasegmental, syntactic and lexical levels of his poetic texts. The effect for the reader is obvious. It creates an artistic experience in which the reader must provide the missing or unmentioned element and integrate it with that which is presented on the surface level of the text in order to derive meaning. Therefore, what is not stated explicitly becomes a part of the text and engenders reader collaboration in the creative process. Meaning, however, becomes a moving target, since each individual reader must provide the missing element and arrive at a particular conclusion, a conclusion inevitably undermined by language's inherent inconsistencies. In addition, González frequently alters the traditional Hegelian formula of thesis-antithesis-synthesis to suit his own needs.[7] Instead of presenting the thesis from which the antithesis may be generated, the poet more often presents first the antithesis – in the form of unorthodox or 'anti-poetic' elements, negative assertions, contrary-to-fact statements, speakers who adopt an ironic or parodic tongue-in-cheek posture – from which the reader must derive the underlying thesis and intent of the text at hand.[8]

The most obvious manifestation of the dialectic between presence and absence is the already well-documented use by González of irony and parody in communicating a meaning that goes beyond the surface level of the text.[9] Benson ably demonstrates how through the shifting, ironic voices of unreliable narrators the poet is able to communicate the absolute relativity of surrounding reality. Since no one speaker will accept responsibility, the onus of integrating and resolving the various views of reality falls upon the reader, who frequently must bring to bear intertextual resonances and extraneous experiences not explicitly mentioned on the surface level of the text.[10] Therefore, presence is defined by absence. Those elements not readily available on the surface level must be conjured up by the reader and accommodated as a central component in the text. Paradoxically, that which is marginal – the absent element – becomes the principal defining characteristic of the supposedly complete present element. The speaker draws the reader into the text by delegating the responsibility of mediation between those present and absent elements.

The poem entitled "Discurso a los jóvenes" (*SE* 115-117) demonstrates González's able and compelling use of ironic discourse. The speaker in this text is a rather pompous after-dinner orator who exhorts the young to shun intelligent reasoning, thought, and individual responsibility:

> Tú, Piedra,
> hijo de Pedro, nieto
> de Piedra
> y biznieto de Pedro,
> esfuérzate
> para ser siempre piedra mientras vivas,
> para ser pedro Petrificado Piedra Blanca,
> para no tolerar el movimiento. (11.22-29)

Their sights should be set on maintaining the *status quo*, even to the detriment of those individual rights necessary for a free society: "Fuego para quemar lo que lo frece. / Hierro para aplastar lo que se alza" (11.42-43). His final criticism is directed at "los que sueñen, / a los que no buscan / más que luz y verdad, / a los que deberían ser humildes / y a veces no lo son, así es la vida" (11.56-60). The duty and subsequent honor of the young lie not in their individual potential and worth but rather in obeying without question the command of their leaders. In return, the speaker promises them "paz y patria feliz, / orden, / silencio" (11.68-70).[11] The speaker has presented this comic yet tragic scene in completely ironic terms. The reader, of course, discerns that this scene represents the poet's critical view of a politically repressive environment. His views are the exact opposite of those expressed by the orator and enter into the fabric of the text because of the sense of outrage evoked in the reader. The poet demands that the reader take as the point of departure the opposite view of that expressed on the surface level of the text by the overbearing orator. Thus, the absent element provided by the reader, namely, a heralding of free speech, individual responsibilities, and the right to protest against any form of repression, is combined with the view present in the text to bring about the ironic discourse. Other critics have noted that González attempts to reconcile an absent, idyllic past or future with a less-than-perfect present.[12] This pairing of the past and/or future with the present is frequently expressed through a syntactical style that blurs or decenters the speaker's specific point of departure. One such surface-level feature that emphasizes the dialectic of presence versus absence is González's use of contrary-to-fact and *if* clauses. The word *if* may denote a potential condition or hypothetical supposition.[13] By utilizing a contrary-to-fact statement the speaker draws attention to the vast difference between the verbalized portrait in his text and the contrasting reality against which he is reacting. This common reality is of secondary importance and therefore is for the most part absent; the imagined vista is present before the reader's eyes and becomes more real. Thus, the absent reality is 'unrealized', while the present conjuration is bestowed with physical substance, albeit in linguistic form. The reader must synthesize and create a balanced vision of both the present and absent elements in the contrary-to-fact statements. By way of illustration, in the poem "El recuerdo" (*SE* 78) the speaker attempts to describe a mesmerizing memory of the past. He never specifies whether this memory refers to a woman, a difficult human relationship, or perhaps even his own poetic voice. The poem begins:

> Si fuese débil, si
> me abandonase a tu canto un solo instante,
> no podría
> desasirme ya nunca de tus redes
> 5 y me debatiría,
> inmóvil en tu centro.
> los siglos o las horas que aún me quedan.
>
> Te oigo a lo lejos,
> hablas,
> 10 de cosas que también están lejanas,
> pero no escucho,
> cierro mis oídos,
> y miro el mar, el cielo, las gaviotas
> con toda la atención puesta en su vuelo,
> 15 con toda el alma sobre su aventura.
> . . .

The allusions of this poem, of course, are in reference to Ulysses' encounter with the sirens: the song that attracts him, the sea's ambiance, the passage of time, and the speaker's determination not to fall prey to the captivating yet potentially fatal attraction.[14] In using a contrary-to-fact statement, the speaker encourages the reader to integrate three quite distinct levels of reality: first, that which is most evident, namely, the alluring reality presented in the poetic text 'as if' it were true; second, the tedious reality against which he is reacting; and third, the far-distant mythical reality of Homer's saga. The effectiveness of the opening contrary-to-fact statement is reinforced in several ways later on in the poem. In the second stanza the speaker emphasizes his distance, both physical and volitional, by mentioning that distance, "Te oigo *a lo lejos*, / hablas / de cosas que también están *lejanas*" (11.8-10); he also affirms his denial of the contrary-to-fact statement through the use of a conjunction and negation, "*pero no* escucho, / cierro mis oídos" (11.11-12). The opening verse of the third stanza also offers a reiteration of this firm stance of denial:

> No tienes fuerzas para detenerme,
> pero
> cada vez que te oigo a pesar mío,
> vacilo
> 20 y siento
> el deseo de acostarme
> sobre la arena blanca de la playa
> y llorar escuchando tus historias
> que empiezan de mil modos diferentes
> 25 para llegar al mismo
> final siempre:
>
> "el hombre, solo, frente al mar, por último . . ."

But immediately following this statement of resoluteness, in line 16 above, the speaker begins to hedge. His hesitation is marked not only by his semantic orientation but also by the variation in verse length: "pero / cada vez que te oigo a pesar mío, / vacilo / y siento / el deseo de acostarme / sobre la arena blanca de la playa." At this point the speaker demands that the reader make a subtle yet significant change in the ordering of present and absent levels of reality. The contrary-to-fact reality presented in the first stanza now seems much more plausible; its 'as if' conjecturing has been converted to the common reality of the poet's – and reader's – experience. The tedious reality of the opening lines of verse has faded and become the absent component, whereas the invoked reality of union with a beautiful bygone memory and that of Homer's lyrical creation have come to the forefront. By recognizing his human limitations the speaker facilitates the reader's synthesis of the various levels of reality in the text. The historical presence of the Homeric saga is made more immediate to the reader by the speaker's change in perspective. At the end of the poem, the perception of these levels of reality is completely reversed: that which was closest at the beginning has now become the farthest point of reference. Once more it falls within the reader's ken to convert the absent into the present, and the present into the absent. Both poles of the dialectic are indispensable in the creative process of Angel González. The meaning of the text is this very process of dialectical interchange between presence and absence, whose operation depends on the reader's participation.

González's unique stylistic signature on the lexical, syntactic, and suprasegmental levels exploits language's ability to state, contradict, imply and evolve a certain message. The poet takes advantage of language's seeming inability to express truth directly. The inexorable polysemy that results is broadened still further by the collaboration of the reader in the artistic process. Through such rhetorical strategems as intertextual references, multiple and ironic speakers, and apostrophe, the reader necessarily becomes intimately involved in creating meaning in the text. Through the interplay of present and absent elements, the *différance* mentioned earlier, the poet encourages the reader to use the text that appears on the printed page merely as a starting point. Meaning is derived only when the reader brings into play those elements provided by the poet along with those coming from the reader's personal experience and suggested by the resonances emanating from the text. This dynamic dialectical relationship of present and absent elements is manifested on the syntactical, lexical and suprasegmental levels of Angel González's poetic texts. It bestows universality upon this poet's work, since each reader has the opportunity to interject a personal component into the literary text. But it also is a mark of the poet's own unique artistic creativity, one that is able to capture handily and precisely the mercurial and capricious nature of twentieth-century existence. Ultimately, this dialectic of presence and absence may be a sign of the poet's interpretation of life, humanity's position within a constantly changing world, the poet's relationship to art, and to language itself. Each of these relationships must be defined as an unending and dynamic process of interaction between present and past, object and context, sender and receiver. Thus, the social thrust of González's poetry cannot be disjoined from the code in which it is communicated. His poetic texts demand an active role of those who receive them on both a linguistic and thematic plane and also enjoin those readers to enter into a dialogue with culture itself.

NOTES

[1]See, for example, the studies by José Olivio Jiménez, "De la poesía social a la poesía crítica: a propósito de *Tratado de urbanismo* (1967), de Angel González," in his *Diez años de poesía española* 281-304; Tino Villanueva,

"*Aspero mundo*, de Angel González: de la contemplación lírica a la realidad histórica," *Journal of Spanish Studies: Twentieth Century* 8 (1980): 161-80; Florentino Martino, "La poesía de Angel González," *Papeles de Son Armadans* 57, no. 171 (1970): 229-47.

In the preparation of this study I used González's *Palabra sobre palabra*, 2nd ed. (1968; Barcelona: Barral, 1977). From this point forward all page citations will be listed in the body of the text. The abbreviation *SE* represents *Sin esperanza, con convencimiento*, one of the poet's individual collections reprinted in the comprehensive *Palabra sobre palabra*.

[2]Jiménez 281-85; Douglas K. Benson, "La ironía, la función del hablante y la experiencia del lector en la poesía de Angel González," *Hispania* 64, no. 4 (1981): 570.

[3]Many other studies have signaled already the importance of the reader in relation to Angel González's poetry. See especially the studies by Douglas Benson, including the previously mentioned "La ironía," as well as his "Linguistic Parody and Reader Response in the Worlds of Angel González," *Anales de la literatura española contemporánea* 7 (1982): 11-30; Andrew P. Debicki, *Poetry of Discovery* 59-80; and Martino.

[4]Jonathan Culler, *On Deconstruction: Theory and Criticism after Structuralism* (Ithaca: Cornell University Press, 1982) 95.

[5] Culler 103.

[6]For a general theoretical introduction to deconstruction and its implications for the study of literature, see the books by Culler, Christopher Norris, *Deconstruction: Theory and Practice* (New York: Methuen, 1982), and John Sturrock, ed., *Structuralism and Since* (New York: Oxford University Press, 1979). Barbara Johnson, *The Critical Difference* (Baltimore: Johns Hopkins University Press, 1980) contains a series of essays that apply the deconstructivist perspective to literature.

[7]Gary A Singleterry, in his unpublished Ph.D. dissertation entitled "The Poetic Cosmovision of Angel González" (University of New Mexico, 1972), utilized the dialectic method, but on a purely thematic level.

[8]See especially Debicki 59-80.

[9]Studies of Angel González's use of irony are numerous. See especially those by Benson and Martino.

[10]Benson, "La ironía," especially 570-75.

[11]González's irony becomes more caustic in his later collections of verse. See, for example, "Alocución a los veintitrés," a poem from *Grado elemental*.

This text describes a situation similar to that of "Discurso a los jóvenes." The former poem has been treated by Debicki (70-71).

[12]See Debicki and Jiménez.

[13]Emilio M. Martínez Amador, *Diccionario gramatical* (Barcelona: Editorial Ramón Sopena, 1953) 987.

[14]Homer, *The Odyssey*, trans. W.H.D. Rouse (New York: New American Library, 1937) Book XII. "First you will come to the Sirens, who bewitch every one who comes near them. If any man draws near in his innocence and listens to their voice, he never sees home again, never again will wife and little children run to greet him with joy; but the Sirens bewitch him with their melodious song. There in a meadow they sit, and all around is a great heap of bones, mouldering bodies and withering skins. Go on past that place, and do not let the men hear; you must knead a good lump of wax and plug their ears with pellets. If you wish to hear them yourself, make the men tie up your hands and feet and fasten your body tight to the mast, and then you can enjoy the song as much as you like. Tell them that if you shout out and command them to let you loose, they must tie you tighter with a few more ropes" (129-30).

THE LUDIC POETRY OF ANGEL GONZÁLEZ

Martha LaFollette Miller
University of North Carolina at Charlotte

Angel González's poetry begins to undergo a significant transformation in the late sixties. At that time, González says, he began to base his poems more on schemes than on experiences and to tend increasingly towards the joke, towards verbal play, and towards parody.[1] He thus intensified his incursions into what Susan Stewart, in *Nonsense: Aspects of Intertextuality in Folklore and Literature*, identifies as the "ludic genres."[2]

The ludic elements in González's poetry take a variety of forms, and Stewart's ideas provide a helpful background for understanding González's ludic texts. As she points out, ludic texts bear "paradoxical messages regarding their own existence" (39). They violate common-sense interpretive procedures, "either by presenting paradoxes of framing, or by juxtaposing two or more universes of discourse and thereby erasing a common-sense context ..." (39). Thus they are created when two incompatible provinces of meaning, each having its own set of rules for interpretation, are brought together within the same frame, or when a metatextual message conflicts with a textual one. For Stewart, the procedures that create ludic texts are intertextual because they are based on systems of classification. And they "tend toward nonsense," which, according to Stewart, makes them both critical and self-critical; as she puts it, "[n]onsense as a critical activity is and is about change; is an aspect of and is about the ongoing nature of social process" (200).

It is obvious from the above that metafictional elements often play an important role in the creation of ludic texts.[3] Stewart explains the relationship between metafiction and nonsense as follows:

> Metafiction traverses and manipulates not only the domain of common sense, but the domains of other kinds of fictions as well. Its violation of common-sense principles of order, its foregrounding of the cultural nature of signification, its exposure of systems of interpretation as systems, its comments upon the nature of communicative modes, give it its status as a metafiction — a fiction about fictions — a fiction necessarily about itself. (21)

Any metafictional text, because its context is "impossible, hermetic, a place that cannot happen that is the fiction itself" (21) is, Stewart suggests, intimately connected with nonsense.

Those familiar with González's 1977 volume *Muestra, corregida y aumentada, de algunos procedimientos narrativos y de las actitu-*

des sentimentales que habitualmente comportan will recall that he entitles a whole section of that book "Metapoesía." Yet a glance at his works as a whole reveals a tendency towards metapoetic textual play from the very beginning. "Me falta una palabra," from his first book, *Aspero mundo* (1956), parodies the stereotypically Juanramonian aestheticism of the poet who tries to exclude the world while seeking the word, unaware that the world has in fact given him the word. Because of its first-person speaker, the poem is not just González's criticism of the aesthete who shuns social concerns, but is also a ludic text in which play consists of the contradiction between its speaker's statement that his utterance is not a poem and the fact that his very statement makes up a poetic text. Or, as Stewart would say, a negative statement made on one level implies a contradictory metastatement on another. The speaker denies the existence of a poem, but the reader sees in the combination of speaker's voice and authorial super-voice a poem about poetry-making, a poem within a poem. "Me falta una palabra" also plays with the notion of authorial intentionality and raises questions of the reader's role, in a sense undermining its own anti-aestheticism, since it is itself a poem about aesthetic matters as much as about social questions.

Though present from his first book on, metapoetical play and nonsense assume greater importance during the period that begins with the publication of *Tratado de urbanismo* in 1967. This is a period which, as we saw earlier, González views as a transitional stage in his development. "A veces," from *Breves acotaciones para una biografía* (1969) (*Palabra sobre palabra* 257), offers a textual paradox similar to the one found in "Me falta una palabra." Again the speaker is a poet; comparing writing verse to sexual intercourse, he complains that, like orgasms, poems just won't come sometimes. For confirmation he quotes César Vallejo, then states that of course Vallejo was lying:

> Lo expresaba muy bien César Vallejo:
> "Lo digo, y no me corro."
>
> Pero él disimulaba

Like Epimenides the Cretan, who emerged from a cave to state that all Cretans were liars, this speaker casts doubt, with his final assertion, on his own words; through raising the possibility that Vallejo's text may be a lie, he suggests that he too may be lying, leaving his reader suspended midway between belief and disbelief.

"La paloma" (from *Tratado de urbanismo*, 1967 [*Poemas: Edición del autor* 132]), exhibits a different sort of intertextual nonsense. The poem is a collage of elements related to each other largely arbitrarily. Snatches of the Mexican song "La paloma" alternate with reportage on the history of sightings of the rare bird, hope, glimpsed in various parts of the world associated with resistance and revolution, most recently in a Southeast Asian rice paddy. González claims the poem, which dates from the Vietnam era, as one of his most political, though he states that when he wrote it, his despair at the uselessness of words had led him, at least on a conscious level, to cultivate poetry with no transcendence at all ("Introducción," *Poemas: Edición del autor* 21). Even though part of the poem coheres as an exhortative political message, the presence of the lyrics of a popular love song within the closed field of the text draws attention to the poetic surface and to the arbitrary generation of the poematic imagery. The distinction between form and content is thus subverted, and the nature of the poem as a fiction is highlighted. To borrow Marjorie Perloff''s terminology, we might say that "La paloma" is characterized by "unmediated presentation" and by indeterminacy. Like much recent poetry it remains, at least in part, an indecipherable enigma; its poetic surface takes precedence over its function as the communication of an epiphany or higher reality.[4]

Though the above examples confirm the presence of a metapoetic strain in González's poetry from the beginning, it is in the 1970s that his tendency towards metapoetry fully blossoms. In this he coincides with other poets of his generation and, perhaps more importantly, with historical trends of that moment.[5] Several critics have noted this fact, and particular mention must be made of Nancy Mandlove's fine analysis of "Calambur" from *Muestra*, which she terms "a metapoetic pun — full of intertextual echoes and revitalized conventions. ..."[6] During this period González creates several poems that take as their subject the genres to which they supposedly belong. Such poems are ludic because they telescope form and content onto the same plane, thus blurring the distinction between a class and its members. "Elegía pura" (157), from *Muestra*, as an elegy devoid of content, evokes all the traditions of its genre but violates its principle of commemoration of something beyond the poem. Similarly, "Egloga" (148-49), from *Procedimientos narrativos*, supposedly a pastoral poem, is in reality "about" the conventions of the pastoral genre.[7]

Another poem from the same period, "Dato biográfico" (*Muestra* [*Poemas: Edición del autor* 176-77]), creates intertextual nonsense through the juxtaposition of incompatible discourses of meaning. In describing the cockroaches in his apartment in terms more properly applicable to an inferior social class than to a zoological one, González confuses human and subhuman categories, social and scientific classificatory systems, and literal and figurative planes. Here, as in the poems mentioned above, intertextuality plays a key role, though the texts evoked, rather than literary works, are clichés from social discourse, applied in contradiction to common-sensical rules of interpretation.

A detailed analysis of one of González's most recent poems reveals continued insistence on the creation of intertextual nonsense. "Avanzaba de espaldas aquel río. . . ," unpublished until the 1980 anthology *Poemas: edición del autor*, wavers between reference and "compositional game."[8] The poem presents a river's seaward advance as a quintessential Romantic farewell scene, complete with nearly every cliché such scenes entail: a crepuscular autumnal setting, tender handclasps, glistening eyes that caress what they must leave behind:

1 Avanzaba de espaldas aquel río.
2 No miraba adelante, no atendía
3 a su Norte — que era el Sur.
4 Contemplaba los álamos
5 altos, llenos de sol, reverenciosos,
6 perdiéndose despacio cauce arriba.
7 Se embebía en los cielos
8 cambiantes
9 del otoño:
10   decía adiós a su luz.
11 Retenía un instante las ramas de los sauces
12 en sus espumas frías,
13 para dejarlas irse — o sea, quedarse — ,
14 mojadas y brillantes, por la orilla.
15 En los remansos
16 demoraba su marcha,
17 absorto ante el crepúsculo.

18 No ignoraba al mar ácido, tan próximo
19 que ya en el viento su rumor se oía.
20 Sin embargo,
21 continuaba avanzando de espaldas aquel río,
22 y se ensanchaba
23 para tocar las cosas que veía:
24 los juncos últimos,
25 la sed de los rebaños,
26 las blancas piedras por su afán pulidas.
27 Si no podía alcanzarlo,
28 lo acariciaba todo con sus ojos de agua.

29 ¡Y con qué amor lo hacía!

The heavy intertextual resonances of "Avanzaba de espaldas aquel río. . ." are inescapable. The poem, like "Me falta una palabra," evokes a Juanramonian aesthetic; the heavy-handed personification of nature and the pathetic fallacy recall Jiménez's earliest books, as a comparison with the following passage, from "Otoñal" (*Ninfeas*, 1900), reveals:[9]

Obscuros nublados manchaban el cielo;
el Sol moribundo se hundía en Ocaso,
de rojo sudario cubierto . . .;

. . . .

el río lanzaba rumor somnolento,
besando la orilla al dormirse,
con ósculos tiernos;

. . . .

      ¡Qué tarde más triste . . .!

. . . .

El valle y el monte y el río y el cielo
estaban vestidos de luto . . .,
y su alma y la mía vestidas de negro . . .

. . . .

. . . Tenía en mis manos sus manos heladas,
mi pálida frente en su pecho . . .;

. . . .

In "Avanzaba de espaldas aquel río. . . ," then, González picks up one of the underlying threads of his own poetry — the elegiac mode — in order to parody it. The poem recalls not only Juan Ramón, but also the traditional image of human lives as rivers en route to the sea that is death; the river's depiction as a person reluctantly walking backwards and caressing with his eyes all that he is leaving suggests a prolonged and heartfelt good-bye in the face of permanent separation. The poem in fact recalls "Por aquí pasa un río" from González's first book, *Aspero mundo*, which implicitly compares a human life to the course of a river. Yet unlike that poem and other traditional poetry, here the elegiac text is undermined by various forms of verbal play. Metaphor becomes a personification so extreme that it oversteps the limits of what common sense can accept. The poem thus attains burlesque proportion through its exaggeration of traditional poetic techniques.

Throughout the poem, word play that draws attention to the surface of the text or to the literal/figurative duality consistently undermines the pathos of the river's fateful progress. The juxtaposition of literal and figurative meanings, and in fact their actual contradiction of one another, appear first in the opening line, where the anatomical precision of the reference to the river's "espaldas" creates dissent in the reader who, though ready to accept Manrique's conceptual comparison between smaller and larger rivers and men of greater and lesser importance, may find the vision of a river walking backwards ridiculously concrete. And as in other instances throughout the poem, contradictory wording — here the phrase "avanzaba de espaldas," in which the river that is said to be advancing forwards seems more properly to be withdrawing backwards — draws our attention away from the referent and to the poetic surface.[10] (The verb "avanzaba" evokes, as an underlying text, its opposite, "retrocedía".) In line 3, the phrase "su Norte — que era el Sur" likewise juxtaposes literal meaning — actual direction — with the figurative connotations of the word "Norte," continuing the suggestion of unidirectional movement overlaid with bidirectional pull. Similarly, the reference to willow branches that the river retains a moment and then releases "para dejarlas irse — o sea quedarse," in counterposing opposites, draws the reader's attention away from the implications of farewell and towards the more literary question of literal exactness versus figurative sense.

Also undermining the Romantic vision of "Avanzaba de espaldas aquel río. . ." is the presence of a series of terms that though figuratively applicable to good-bye scenes belong to a scientific semantic field that refers to water. In lines 7 and 8, where the river "Se embebía / en los cielos / cambiantes / de otoño," the literal suggestion of evaporation undercuts the figurative vision of the river as gazing, transfixed, at the sky. The image, in lines 11 and 12, of the river retaining the willow branches in its water — "Retenía un instante las ramas de los sauces / en sus espumas frías" — echoes the cliché, seen in Juan Ramón Jiménez above, of the tender farewell handclasp, the word "espumas" serving here to substitute for the word "manos," though both can be read literally as well. That the river slows its course in the eddies receives intentional significance, in lines 15 through 17 ("En los remansos / demoraba su marcha, / absorto ante el crepúsculo"), yet the word "absorto," like "retener" and "embeberse," forms part of a semantic field that includes such scientific terminology relating to aquatic behavior as th words absorption, retention, and saturation, and thus its presence has the effect of undercutting the personification of the river. Likewise, the application of the adjectives "mojadas y brillantes," which belong to a semantic field referring to tear-filled eyes, is generated by the botanical name "sauce llorón." The willows, which weep only figuratively in real life, are here presented as literally crying; at the same time, the adjectives "mojadas y brillantes" are literally applicable to willow branches on the riverbank.

This literal/figurative confusion continues until the end of the poem. The verb "ensancharse," applied to the river in line 22, describes a river's widening as it approaches the sea, but in the context of the reference to "las blancas piedras por su afán pulidas," in line 26, it evokes as well the figurative self-satisfaction that seems to infuse the river/person in the last line, converting the river's tragic good-bye into tragicomedy.

The river's final caress, in line 29, again plays upon the literal and the figurative planes: "lo acariciaba todo con sus ojos de agua."

80

A triple-planed pun, the phrase "ojos de agua" evokes the tears of the personified river, expresses metaphorically the water's literal contact with the riverbank as it passes, and, on a more linguistic plane, plays with the set phrase "ojo de agua," signifying spring. This phrase could be considered as having generated the poem, since it implies that water has eyes, and the entire poem is a river's vision of its past.

To conclude, in "Avanzaba de espaldas aquel río..." two different models of nature — the scientific and the Romantic — are set against each other. The poem, in counterposing the Romantic legacy of subjective symbolism to the notion of the power of linguistic conventions, expresses a quintessentially twentieth-century dilemma. Its subject, thus, is not the good-bye itself but rather the literary devices that make up the elegiac tradition.

In contrast to a poem by Machado in which all elements — twilight, autumn, water, for example — "fall together," in the Symbolist manner, fusing and mutually intensifying each other, in a vision that evokes some transcendent mystery,[11] González's poem falls apart as literal and figurative levels conflict. The content of the poem, natural description, coexists with elements that highlight the cultural determination of this content. Given the allusions to a Juanramonian sensibility, we might almost interpret the personification of the river as suggestive of the poet, who, keeping his eyes on past literary tradition, admires the stones, his poems, that he polishes as he passes by. It would probably be too farfetched to interpret the reference to the river's premonition of the sea as an allusion to Juan Ramón's decisive encounter with that entity though, given González's multi-layered irony, such an interpretation is not altogether impossible.

"Avanzaba de espaldas aquel río ..." and the other poems I have examined here tend towards nonsense, not only because they confuse categories, thus calling attention to themselves as texts, but also because, as poems in some sense about poetic devices, they are paradoxical. They are clearly ludic texts, demonstrating Stewart's concept of the ludic work as both critical and self-critical; they are texts that *are* change as well as being *about* change.[12]

NOTES

[1]"Introducción," *Poemas: Edición del autor* (Madrid: Cátedra, 1980) 22. González's books include *Aspero mundo* (Madrid: Ediciones Rialp, 1956); *Sin esperanza con convencimiento* (Barcelona: Literaturasa, 1961); *Grado elemental* (Paris: Ruedo Ibérico, 1962); *Palabra sobre palabra* (Madrid: Poesía Para Todos, 1965); *Tratado de urbanismo* (Barcelona: El Bardo, 1967); *Palabra sobre palabra* (Barcelona: Seix Barral, 1968; 2nd ed. Barral Editores, 1972; rpt. 1977); *Breves acotaciones para una biografia* (Las Palmas de

Gran Canaria: Inventarios Provisionales, 1969); *Procedimientos narrativos* (Santander: La Isla de los Ratones, 1972); *Muestra de algunos procedimientos narrativos y de las actitudes sentimentales que habitualmente comportan* (Madrid: Turner, 1976; 2nd ed., *corregida y aumentada*, 1977); and *Prosemas o menos* (Santander: Colección Clásicos de Todos los Años, 1983). Page numbers in the text refer to *Poemas: Edición del autor* unless otherwise indicated.

[2](Baltimore: The Johns Hopkins University Press, 1979) 39. Page references in the text refer to this volume.

[3]I use the term "metafiction" here in a general sense, to include metapoetic devices.

[4]Marjorie Perloff, *The Poetics of Indeterminacy: Rimbaud to Cage* (Princeton: Princeton University Press, 1981) 28-29. Perloff quotes Roger Cardinal's essay "Enigma," *20th Century Studies* 12 (1974): 42-62. For a discussion of the term "unmediated presentation," which Perloff attributes to Jerome Rothenberg, see 37. Further page references to Perloff will be given parenthetically in the text.

[5]Margaret H. Persin, Andrew P. Debicki, Nancy Mandlove, and Robert Spires, "Metaliterature and Recent Spanish Literature," *Revista Canadiense de Estudios Hispánicos* 7.2 (1983) 297-309. Also see Fanny Rubio and José Luis Falcó, *Poesía española contemporánea; Historia y antología (1939-1980)* (Madrid: Alhambra, 1982) 86-88, for a discussion of metapoetry in this period in the works of such younger poets as Gimferrer, Carnero, and Talens.

[6]Her article, included in "Metaliterature and Recent Spanish Literature," above, is titled "Used Poetry: The Transparent Language of Gloria Fuertes and Angel González."

[7]For a detailed analysis of these poems, see my article, "Literary Tradition versus Speaker Experience in the Poetry of Angel González," *Anales de la literatura española contemporánea* 7.1 (1982), 79-95.

[8]This is characteristic, according to Perloff, of poetry of indeterminacy (34).

[9]Juan Ramón Jiménez, *Primeros libros de poesía*, 3rd ed. (Madrid: Aguilar, 1967) 1499-1501). I am indebted to John Wilcox for pointing out the similarity between González's poems and the early Juan Ramón.

[10]Terry Eagleton (*Literary Theory: An Introduction* [Minneapolis: University of Minnesota Press, 1983] 15) points out that in our culture we view ourselves as moving forwards into the future, although in at least one other culture, people are considered to move backwards into the future.

[11]See Perloff (29-30) for a discussion of the integration characteristic of Symbolism and Modernism versus the disintegration of poetry of indeterminacy. The characterization of Modernism as a "falling together" is James McFarlane's (from "The Mind of Modernism," *Modernism 1840-1930*, ed. Malcolm Bradbury and James McFarlane, Pelican Guides to English Literature [New York: Penguin Books, 1976] 92), quoted by Perloff.

[12]This work was supported in part by funds from the Foundation of The University of North Carolina at Charlotte and from the State of North Carolina.

WRITING AND READING:
DIALECTICAL CORRELATIVES IN
FRANCISCO BRINES' *INSISTENCIAS EN LUZBEL*

Judith Nantell
University of Arizona

Francisco Brines' contemplative and philosophical poetry has established him as one of Spain's most highly acclaimed and influential contemporary poets. Concerned primarily with the themes of mortality and temporality, Brines' *Las brasas* (1960), *El Santo inocente* (1965), *Palabras a la oscuridad* (1966), *Aún no* (1971), and *Insistencias en Luzbel* (1977)[1] analyze and assess modern man's attempts to confront and comprehend the enigma of existence. Brines' sustained investigation into and original interpretation of what he refers to as the "oculta verdad"[2] of existence has led Carlos Bousoño, Spain's leading literary critic and theorist, himself a noted poet, to conclude that "Brines se nos ofrezca como el poeta metafísico por excelencia *de su generación*" (P 35).

Born in 1932, Brines is a member of the Spanish Generation of 1956-71 which includes, according to Andrew Debicki, such poets as Angel Crespo, Gloria Fuertes, Jaime Gil de Biedma, Angel González, Manuel Mantero, Claudio Rodríguez, Carlos Sahagún, and José Angel Valente. One of the significant and distinguishing characteristics of the works of this group of Spanish poets is, as Debicki points out in *Poetry of Discovery, The Spanish Generation of 1956-71*, "the stress placed on poetry as an act of discovery and knowledge rather than mere communication." For these poets, the poem becomes "a vehicle for a creative but necessarily incomplete journey of discovery, a journey in which both speaker and reader participate and in which the language of the text does not always provide definitive answers."[3]

In discussing the nature of poetry, Brines has explained that he values a poetry that "se ejercita con afán de conocimiento." By means of and with the aid of this more cognitive poetry "el poeta trata de conocer, de indagar una oculta verdad ... este afán de conocer se aplica sobre las muy extensas zonas del misterio que todavía nos circundan, y de las que se saben pocas cosas con claridad. En esta tarea, en este esfuerzo, veo una dignificación del poeta, quien, a su vez, es el primer destinatario del nuevo conocimiento."[4]

This attitude regarding poetry as a means both to decipher and to know the "oculta verdad" of existence is shared by many of the poets of Brines' generation. Carlos Sahagún, for example, explains that the poem is an "indagación en lo oscuro mediante la cual, una vez terminado el poema, el poeta conocerá la realidad desde otras perspectivas."[5] Regarding the poetic process, José Angel Valente stresses: "De ahí que el proceso de la creación poética sea un movimiento de indagación y tanteo en que la identificación de cada nuevo elemento modifica a los demás o los elimina, porque todo poema es un conocimiento haciéndose."[6] For these poets, as well as for others of their generation, *writing* poetry is of paramount importance because, as each comes to learn while engaged in the creative act, by writing the poet is able to decipher and comprehend the enigma that he/she has set out to explain by means of poetic discourse.

My discussion will focus on Brines' important collection, *Insistencias en Luzbel*, as poetry representative of his generation's quest for knowledge through poetry. I shall demonstrate that, for Brines, the creative act is coincident with the cognitive act of unraveling the ontological mystery that is the subject of his poems. The poet's journey toward knowledge of the enigma of existence is, however, an "incomplete journey of discovery," to borrow Debicki's observation, since, as will be shown, it relies upon a reader who will first participate in and then complete the incomplete acts of existing and creating initiated by the poet in the poem. For Brines, writing poetry is not only a "method of knowing;"[7] it is also an overt appeal to the reader to collaborate in the ontological, creative and cognitive processes begun by the poem.

Briefly looking at *Insistencias en Luzbel* as a unified whole, the cryptic philosophical poetry of Brines' 1977 collection[8] presents the reader with a series of ontological poem-portraits where various poetic speakers, engaged in intellectual and emotional crises, ponder and seek to know the meaning of self-conscious, personal existence. Concerned with the most significant and perhaps the most perplexing of all ontological problems, the meaning of Being, poetry becomes Brines' method for approaching, disclosing and, ultimately, comprehending the multiple and complex facets of this problem.

In the poetry of *Insistencias en Luzbel*, Brines reformulates and originally interprets the modes of authentic and unauthentic Being investigated by Martin Heidegger in *Sein und Zeit*.[9] The various poetic personae of Brines' collection are engaged in a dialectic as they either authentically accept the possibility of personal death or unauthentically deny this ontological potentiality, instead conniving to deceive themselves about their ultimate finitude. The speaker of "Epitafio del vivo" (50), for example, acknowledges the inevitability of death and accepts the fact that "Soy misterioso: sufro, y no me quedo" (l. 1). The speaker of "Definición de la nada" (16) further discovers that the meaning of non-Being is known only by living, by Being-towards the potential impossibility of existence: "Lo pensáis como un frío, mas esa es vuestra carne. / No afirma y nada niega su firme coherencia" (ll. 10-11). In "Desde el error" (25), however, the poet depicts man in the unauthentic mode of Being:

Creamos el olvido, pues manchamos la nada.
Entre dos inocencias, el engaño.
Entre la nada y el olvido, nadie.   (ll. 12-14)

Another prophetic voice of the collection further reveals the "Actos de supresión" (23-24) in which human Being is often engaged as it seeks to forget its important aim of becoming:

Fértil o estéril, ¿qué más da? Ardiente
es el engaño. Y esto somos: torpes
ensayos, en las sombras, de una argucia.
Un maltrecho final:
vanas repeticiones del olvido.   (ll. 23-27)

The poetic sketches of modern man displayed throughout *Insistencias en Luzbel* not only reveal multiple aspects of the poet's own ontological inquiry into the *nada/olvido* dialectic but also, as is characteristic of literature inspired by existential philosophy, invite the reader to synthesize the dialectical view of existence disclosed in the text.

Brines' inquiry into the modes of authentic Being and unauthentic Being in *Insistencias en Luzbel* differs from that developed by Heidegger in that the poet's assumed personae do not always seek to know nor willingly accept the possibility of personal death. Many speakers of *Insistencias en Luzbel* not only recognize but also advocate the positive, even beneficial, results of living in the unauthentic mode of existence. These speakers espouse various "insistencias en el engaño" (33), as the poet has so aptly entitled the second section of his book of poetry. The "engaño" disclosed in these poems is that of human Being's desire to deceive itself into believing that it is not death-bound.[10] Often, therefore, Brines portrays human Being in the existential mode of continually fabricating the fraud of its existence, thereby seeking "to forget" (the term is both Brines' and Heidegger's)[11] the possibility of its own non-Being.

Throughout *Insistencias en Luzbel* the speakers of Brines' poems, while involved in the process of discovering the meaning of Being, learn to develop strategies that will help them to comprehend the *nada/olvido* dialectic underlying their existence. I will limit my discussion to a representative poem of the collection, "Al lector" (37),[12] and to the actions and stratagems of a particular poetic voice that is often heard, that of the poet/speaker.[13] In the poem "Al lector" the poet/speaker, while analyzing the meaning of existence by means of and with the aid of the poem that he is writing, makes a significant discovery: he comes to know the purpose and the potential both of his existence and of his creative act. Writing itself, therefore, becomes a strategy or a method not only for deciphering and comprehending the enigma of existence but also for initiating and exploiting the possibilities of the text.

Brines' ontological investigation leads the poet, through his poet/speaker persona, to explore and appreciate the role that poetic discourse plays in formulating, literally giving form to, the otherwise amorphous enigma of existence. For Brines the very verbalization of the enigma is itself not only a poetic but also an inventive or constitutive process whereby the poet creates and only thereby discovers the reason for Being. The language of poetry is, then, his unique medium for incarnating and revealing the "oculta verdad."

The poet/speaker of "Al lector" also comes to know another important aspect of the purpose of his existence and of his creation. While engaged in the act of writing poetry he learns that by writing he makes an appeal to the reader to continue the ontological and creative tasks that he has begun. This appeal, in fact, emerges as a strategy used by the poet/speaker of various poems of the collection. In Brines' obscure portrayal of the meaning of existence, the poet, through his assumed poetic persona, openly invites the reader first "to decipher" (13), as a voice urges at the outset of the collection, and then produce the meaning of the text. By means of the reader's response to this appeal and the reader's subsequent participation in the production and elucidation of "the potential meanings of the text"[14] the reader of *Insistencias en Luzbel* comes to know the meaning of Being *and* the meaning of reading and the "ideational activity," to use Wolfgang Iser's term,[15] in which he/she is engaged. Reading itself thus becomes a device that the poet of *Insistencias en Luzbel* openly encourages and directly relies upon in order to attain the possibilities of Being and writing that are yet to be realized.

Recent reader-response theories, especially those set forth by Wolfgang Iser, form the underpinnings of my study of the reader's role in Brines' *Insistencias en Luzbel*. Iser's theories regarding the act of reading, the implied reader, and text-reader interaction are especially relevant.[16] According to Iser, the meaning of the text is something that the reader has to assemble and co-create.[17] In Brines' poetry, however, the reader must not only engage in the act of co-creating the meaning of the text but he/she must also engage in the act of creating the potential meaning of the poet's own existence disclosed in the ontological inquiry that is *Insistencias en Luzbel*.

Jean-Paul Sartre's observations concerning "the literary work as an appeal" are also especially relevant to the roles of writing and reading in Brines' *Insistencias en Luzbel*. Sartre writes:

Since creation can find its fulfillment only in reading, since the artist must entrust to another the job of carrying out what he has begun, since it is only through the consciousness of the reader that he can regard himself as essential to his work, all literary work is an appeal. To write is to make an appeal to the reader that he lead into objective existence the revelation which I have undertaken by means of language . . . The writer appeals to the reader's freedom to collaborate in the production of his work.[18]

In "Al lector" Brines calls attention to both writing as an appeal and also what this appeal entails. The first-person speaker of the poem, who is also the poet/speaker or author/speaker, discovers that writing and reading are interdependent acts, and only by means of the reciprocal process of "aliento-alientas" (ll. 4-6) will the potentialities of the creative act and of personal existence be actualized:

1 En las manos el libro.
   Son palabras que rasgan el papel
   desde el dolor o la inquietud que soy,
   ahora que todavía aliento bajo tu misma noche,
5 desde el dolor o la inquietud que fui,
   a ti que alientas debajo de la noche
   y ya no estoy.
   Crees que me percibes en estas manchas negras del
      papel,
   en ese territorio, ya no mío, de la desolación.

10 Las saqué del vacío,
   pude mudarlas por silencio,
   y ahora serían ellas el espejo de mí, no de vosotros.
   Esta es mi herencia sórdida,
   fue un gesto que amé en otros, y en ellos aprendí
15 este vicio secreto que os transmito,
   por si el dolor que padecéis no os fuese suficiente,
   o acaso preciséis de un dolor que pervive sin carne.

   Agotadme, cegadme con vosotros, en la muerte que os
      habrá de llegar,
   y decidme, si acaso lo sabéis, ¿quién nos hizo?

"Al lector," like all of the poems of *Insistencias en Luzbel*, is a highly introspective, ontological investigation of the origin and purpose of Being and also what constitutes Being. Pain, suffering, the *angst* of existence, to borrow Heidegger's term,[19] have as their source the speaker's own recognition of the possibility of personal mortality. The poet/speaker of "Al lector" writes "desde el dolor o la inquietud que soy . . . / desde el dolor o la inquietud que fui . . . / y ya no estoy" (ll. 3, 5, 7). He comprehends that the figurative "territorio . . . de la desolación" (l. 9) of his own existence one day no longer will be his because, as he learns while living, existence is an unavoidable progression toward death: "y ya no estoy ... / Crees que me percibes en estas manchas negras del papel, / en ese territorio, ya no mío, de la desolación" (ll. 7-9). Understanding but nevertheless not willing to accept the possibility of his own finitude, the poet/speaker of this poem, and others of the collection, develops stratagems, both in life and in the text, that will enable him to alter, even if only temporarily, the reality of his death-bound existence.

This poem, however, is also an investigation into the origin and purpose of the creative act and into the role the reader is to play in fulfilling the possibilities of this act. At the outset of "Al lector" the poet/speaker discerns the multiple features constituting both the poem, in particular, and the collection, in general, that he is writing (ll. 1-9). He then begins to question and come to know first the origin of the ideas represented by words "que rasgan el papel" (l. 2), later his own apprenticeship as both a poet and a human Being conscious of personal mortality (ll. 13-14) and, finally, the meaning of the personal mortality about which he writes (ll. 15-17). As the poet/speaker's creative and communicative act draws to an end (ll. 18-19), he comprehends that only by means of this act and the reader's participation in this act will he be able to alter the finiteness both of his Being and of his writing.

For the poet/speaker of "Al lector" the poem is both an object to be perceived, beheld and known and a discourse that represents and reveals personal, existential preoccupations. The collection of poems, "en las manos el libro" (l. 1), "palabras que rasgan el papel" (l. 2), and "estas manchas negras del papel" (l. 8), are all outward forms that collect, contain and, in the case of "words," represent and disclose ("aliento," "transmito," [ll. 4,15]) the poet's inquiry into the meaning of Being and writing.

While engaged in the process of creating and writing the poem, the poet/speaker of "Al lector" discovers that his creative act, like a mirror, fulfills the function of sending back to himself the reflection of his own image, the reflection of his own thoughts:[20] "Las saqué del vacío, pude mudarlas por silencio, y ahora serían ellas el espejo de mí no de vosotros" (ll. 10-12). This reflected image, drawn out of the poet's own "vacío," his own consciousness,[21] his own awareness of the self, his own imagination, is what the reader, now assuming the role of voyeur, has been invited to gaze upon and read at the poet's own request.

The poet's creative act, however, fulfills yet another function in "Al lector." Writing the poem is not only an expressive means of self-analysis but also an inventive means of self-projection. Ironically, by analyzing and recording his personal, ontological possibilities, the poet/speaker comes to know that the poem, and consequently his own personal existence disclosed therein, exists potentially for others, namely the reader(s) addressed in "Al lector."

The poet/speaker heard in this poem and in others of *Insistencias en Luzbel* openly seeks a collaborator, a co-conspirator, a reader who will assume the role of bringing about and carrying out the joint tasks of Being and writing examined in "Al lector." Brines draws attention to the collaborative role of the reader of "Al lector" by directly addressing the reader within the text of his poem. The real or actual reader of "Al lector," who has before him/her this poem and also the entire collection ("en las manos el libro" [l. 1]), thus is offered a particular role to play. This role can perhaps be best understood if Iser's concept of the "implied reader" is used. Iser explains that "this term incorporates both the pre-structuring of the potential meaning of the text, and the reader's actualization of this potential through the reading process."22 In "Al lector," the implied reader, at first the singular *tú* and then the plural *vosotros* addressed (ll. 6-9, 12-19), is a textual construct whose presence in Brines' poem helps to draw attention to and, in fact, elucidate the role that the real reader eventually will play in assembling the meaning of the poem.23

In "Al lector" the poet/speaker not only attempts to comprehend the various facets of both Being and writing but also tries to discern many of the important features of the reader to whom his poem is addressed (ll. 1-9). For this poet/speaker, the reader's act of reading is, in many ways, a reflection and even a re-enactment of the poet's act of writing. Both poet and reader hold and behold the work: "En las manos el libro ... Crees que me percibes en estas manchas negras del papel" (ll. 1, 8). Both poet and reader are also engaged in the reciprocal act of "aliento-alientas" (ll. 4, 6), that is, the act of creating and co-creating the meaning of the poem.

Brines further develops the features of the reader in lines 12-19 of the poem, except here the singular reader addressed in the poem's opening section, the *tú* of lines 4, 6 and 8, has been pluralized into the *vosotros* addressed in lines 10-19. Having established the crucial interdependency of the poet and the reader and also the importance of the reciprocal act of "aliento-alientas," the poet/speaker of "Al lector" now both addresses and seeks the many readers who will read the poem and who will, above all, attempt to heed the poem's final mandates.

In the final two lines of "Al lector" the text's implied reader, the *vosotros* addressed by the speaker, is ordered to perform a specific set of interrelated actions and to supply, ultimately, an answer, or perhaps a series of answers, to the speaker's closing question:

> Agotadme, cegadme con vosotros, en la muerte que os
> habrá de llegar,

y decidme, si acaso lo sabéis, ¿quién nos hizo?
(II. 18-19)

When the speaker urges his addressee to bring about and participate in the actions of "agotadme ... cegadme ... decidme," does this not imply that the poet/speaker of "Al lector" views his personal existence *and* his creative act as incomplete? If so, then his appeal anticipates and is directed to a recipient who will be able and willing to complete the ontological and creative possibilities initiated in "Al lector." The sustained and impassioned plea of the poem's closing moment further clarifies, cleverly brings to the reader's attention, and further helps to draw the reader into the task that awaits him/her in the reading of "Al lector." The reader is asked to continue and to carry out the task begun by the poet's own existential and creative acts.

The presence of such an overt appeal as the one that closes "Al lector" may be startling, especially since the commands and final query of the poem's last lines radically deviate from the more subtle and introspective inquiry into the origin and meaning of Being and writing disclosed earlier. In addition, the poet/speaker rather abruptly, and without warning, mandates the participation of the reader, both the reader addressed and the reader reading the text, for now the two have been exposed, even united, by their task of bringing about what the poet, through his assumed persona, has requested. Earlier in the poem, the speaker's confidant voyeuristically witnessed and listened to the intimate disclosure of the "desolación" underlying his existence and motivating his writing of the poem: "este vicio secreto que os transmito" (l. 15). This confidant has now been asked to relinquish the passive role of listener and to assume, instead, the newly assigned and more active role of completing and explaining the dual acts of existing and writing analyzed in "Al lector." This new role emphasizes not only that writing is an appeal in "Al lector" but also that reading is an act of co-creation, since it is the readers of this poem who, ultimately, will carry out the mandates of "agotadme ... cegadme con vosotros ... decidme" and what these imply, thereby providing an answer to the poem's final question.

The command "agotadme" brings to mind the poem's opening line, "en las manos el libro," and the possibility that this "book," this collection of poems that the writer writes and the reader reads, could one day be "finished," "exhausted," "out of print." By personalizing this mandate and by directing it to someone other than himself, namely the *vosotros* addressed, the poet/speaker highlights the possible finiteness, be it of his "book" of poems (l. 1) or of himself ("y ya no estoy" [l. 7]), that has been the object of his inquiry and the source of his anguish. By means of this command, however, he also underscores the role the reader is to play in bringing about this

90

finitude. The poet/speaker is able to approach and know the possibility of his own mortality only through his readers: "en la muerte que os habrá de llegar" (l. 18). Is not the poet/speaker of "Al lector" suggesting, then, that he confront the possibility of his own non-Being in an unauthentic way, that is, by means of and with the assistance of the death of another? If so, then the poet/speaker has cleverly secured for himself his own form of immortality as long as there are readers who will obey his command. Curiously, however, although the poet/speaker is able to release himself and his poem from the life-death pattern about which he writes, he is not able to release his readers from the possibility of the personal mortality awaiting them. Would this, in itself, not suggest to the poet/speaker that the possibility of non-Being is both inevitable and inexorable?

The complexity of the meaning of Being, it seems, is dismissed in a rather simplistic and unconvincing manner, however, if this interpretation of the view held by the poet/speaker is adopted. Seeking personal finitude only in "la muerte que os habrá de llegar" does not really address the central issue with which the poet/speaker has been concerned throughout "Al lector" and all of *Insistencias en Luzbel*, namely the meaning of self-conscious, personal existence. Another interpretation of the mandate "agotadme" could involve the implication that the poet/speaker's plea is really an urgent request for the readers of his poem to engage in the active process of endlessly trying to "exhaust" the meaning of the ontological inquiry of "Al lector." As long as there are readers of this poem, and others of *Insistencias en Luzbel*, there will be numerous interpretations. As the many readers of "Al lector" are continually drawn into and forever heed the combined commands of "agotadme . . . cegadme con vosotros . . . decidme," each will continue to supply the unwritten portions of the text,[24] each will continue to attempt to exhaust, with his/her own projections, the ontological and interpretive possibilities that are yet to be realized. The implications of the poet/speaker's commands paradoxically point to not the text's exhaustibility, as the reader might first suspect, but rather its inexhaustibility, as the reader comes to learn. Iser's observations regarding the "inexhaustibility of the text" further elucidate what the reader and the poet of "Al lector" come to know:

> One text is potentially capable of several different realizations, and no reading can ever exhaust the full potential, for each individual reader will fill in the gaps in his own way . . . as he reads, he will make his own decision as to how the gap is to be filled . . . By making this decision he implicitly acknowledges the inexhaustibility of the text.[25]

The reciprocal process of writing and reading, Brines' "aliento-alientas," allows the poet/speaker of "Al lector" to secure the existential and interpretative possibilities that he seeks. Brines' appeal "to the reader" thus entails that the reader of "Al lector" bring into existence both the modes of personal existence and the potential meanings of the text that the poet desires but could not possibly have brought about by himself.

Having said what he set out to say, the poet/speaker of "Al lector" urges, in the poem's final line: "decidme, si acaso lo sabéis, ¿quién nos hizo?" His request is direct, and the response he awaits is structured by the seemingly antithetical, thematic elements that the reader identifies, interrelates and finally makes sense of while reading "Al lector." The poet/speaker, by means of his inquiry into personal Being, "soy" / "ya no estoy," and writing "aliento" / "alientas," has sought to understand the dialectic of each. While engaged in his act of Being and his act of writing about Being the poet/speaker, however, discovers not elements in opposition but rather correlative elements that are constantly being preserved and fulfilled by their opposites: "yo-tú," "yo-vosotros," "aliento-alientas," "silencio-transmito," "vacío-palabras."

By means of his act of writing the poet/speaker comes to learn that both this act and the possibility of the personal mortality he has sought to write about and understand are preserved and fulfilled by the reciprocal, regenerative act of reading in which his readers are engaged. The final commands and closing question of "Al lector" underscore the reader's collaborative role not only in this poem but also throughout *Insistencias en Luzbel*. The poet's existential and creative acts both depend on and require the reader's constitutive and interpretive acts if the potential of existence and the potential meanings of the text are to be realized. The poet of "Al lector" writes for his readers ("aliento-alientas") so that these readers might, in turn, tell him ("decidme") of the origin and purpose of his existential and creative acts, thereby completing the incomplete endeavors he has begun.

Brines has thus come to comprehend, by means of his dual inquiry into the meaning of existence and writing, that his existence and his poetry not only are for others but also are fulfilled by others. The reciprocal writing-reading process underlying this poem and the collection that it represents is perhaps best understood if Sartre's observations regarding writing and reading are recalled here:

> The operation of writing implies that of reading as its dialectical correlative and these two connected acts necessitate two distinct agents. It is the conjoint effort of author and reader which brings upon the scene the concrete and imaginary object which is the work of the mind. There is no art except for and by others.[26]

The reader who heeds Brines' appeal in "Al lector" and the numerous *insistencias* of the other poems of the collection will gain knowledge of the potentialities originating in the creative and reciprocal acts of writing and reading. The reader will also discover one other important potentiality that perhaps he/she was unaware of or did not fully comprehend prior to reading the poetry of *Insistencias en Luzbel*. In assembling the meaning of the text, the reader will participate in his/her own introspective analysis of questioning and discovering the purpose of personal existence and ultimately will come to know the potentiality of the self.

The reader of *Insistencias en Luzbel*, for example, may discover that he/she can identify with the existential preoccupations analyzed by Brines in this collection. The reader may even discover that he/she, perhaps, like the poet/speaker of "Al lector," or other voices heard in the collection, has developed his/her own strategies for "forgetting" or avoiding the possibility of personal non-Being. The reader might then learn that human Being's acts of self-deception, Brines' "insistencias en el engaño," are, in fact, patterns of behavior characteristic of human Being. In this way, the interplay of text and reader in Brines' poetry illustrates the Iserian notion that "the production of meaning of literary texts ... does not merely entail the discovery of the unformulated ... it also entails the possibility that we formulate ourselves and so discover what had formerly seemed to elude our consciousness."[27]

The meaning of Being, the fundamental issue underlying all of Francisco Brines' poetry, is deciphered in *Insistencias en Luzbel* by means of the creative, constitutive and cognitive acts of writing and reading. For this poet, the ontological and creative tasks that he has begun, both in living and in writing about existence, are fulfilled by the collaborative and co-creative task of the reader-interpreter of his text. The reader's role as the interpreter of the potential meanings of the text cannot be separated from his/her role as the interpreter of the existential potentialities disclosed by the text since, for Brines, only reading will complete the incomplete acts of Being and writing initiated by the poet of *Insistencias en Luzbel*.[28]

NOTES

[1]Brines' poetic works include *Las brasas* (Madrid: Ediciones Rialp, 1960); *El Santo inocente* (Madrid: Poesía para Todos, 1965); *Palabras a la oscuridad* (Madrid: Insula, 1966); *Aún no* (Barcelona: Ocnos-Editorial Llibres de Sindera, 1971). These were subsequently published in *Poesía 1960-1970*. *Ensayo de una despedida* (Barcelona-Madrid: Plaza de Janés, 1974), where *El Santo inocente* appeared with the new title *Materia narrativa inexacta*. Hereafter, *Poesía 1960-1970* will be abbreviated P when cited. In 1977 Brines published *Insistencias en Luzbel* (Madrid: Visor, 1977). The aforementioned

works were later published in *Poesía 1960-1981. Ensayo de una despedida* (Madrid: Visor, 1984). Brines' recent collections include *Poemas excluidos* (Sevilla: Editorial Renacimiento, 1985); *Selección propia* (Madrid: Cátedra, 1984); *Poemas a D.K.* (Sevilla: El mágico íntimo, 1986); and *El otoño de las rosas* (Sevilla: Editorial Renacimiento, 1986). Important studies of Brines' poetry include: Alejandro Amusco, "Algunos aspectos de la obra poética de Francisco Brines," *Cuadernos Hispanoamericanos* 364 (1979): 52-74; Amusco, "Francisco Brines: Estética de la nada y del sufrimiento," *Insula* 376 (1979): 1 and 12; Douglas K. Benson, "Convenciones de lenguaje y alusiones literarias en la poesía de Francisco Brines' *Insistencias en Luzbel*," *Hispania* 69.1 (1986): 1-11; Benson, "Memory, Tradition and the Reader in the Poetry of Francisco Brines," *MLN* 99 (1984) 308-26; Carlos Bousoño, "Situación y características de la poesía de Francisco Brines," *P* 11-94; Carole Bradford, "The Dialectic of Nothingness in the Poetry of Francisco Brines," *Taller Literario* 1 (1980): 1-12; Bradford, "Francisco Brines and Claudio Rodríguez: Two Recent Approaches to Poetic Creation," *Crítica Hispánica* 2 (1980): 29-40; Andrew P. Debicki, "Francisco Brines: Text and Reader," *Poetry of Discovery. The Spanish Generation of 1956-1971* (Lexington: The University Press of Kentucky, 1982) 20-39; José Olivio Jiménez, "La poesía de Francisco Brines," *Cinco poetas del tiempo* (Madrid: Insula, 1964) 399-458; Jiménez, "Realidad y misterio en *Palabras a la oscuridad* de Francisco Brines," *Diez años de poesía española 1960-1970* (Madrid: Insula, 1972) 175-204; Judith Nantell, "Francisco Brines' *Aún no*: Poetry as Knowledge," *Kentucky Romance Quarterly* 31.5 (1984): 413-24; Nantell, "Modes of Being in Francisco Brines' *Insistencias en Luzbel*," *Revista Canadiense de Estudios Hispánicos* 12 (1988), forthcoming; Margaret H. Persin, "Francisco Brines' *Insistencias en Luzbel*: Toward the Limits of Language and Being," *Recent Spanish Poetry and The Role of the Reader* (Lewisburg, Pa.: Bucknell University Press, 1987) 45-67, also published in Persin, *Poesía como proceso: Poesía española de los Años 50 y 60* (Madrid: José Porrúa Turanzas, 1986) 49-78; Alfonso Sanz Echevarría, "La insistencia de Francisco Brines," *Jugar con fuego: poesía y crítica* 3-4 (1977): 32-49; César Simón, "Algunos aspectos lingüísticos en la sátira de Francisco Brines," *Cuadernos de Filología* (June 1971): 63-70; Luis Antonio de Villena, "Sobre 'Insistencias en Luzbel' y la poesía de Francisco Brines," *Papeles de Son Armadans* 89 (1978): 213-22.

[2]See Brines' "Poética (Notas sobre poesía)" in Antonio Molina, *Poesía española contemporánea. Antología (1939-1964). Poesía cotidiana* (Madrid-Barcelona: Ediciones Alfaguara, 1966) 528.

[3]See Debicki 7-8. In his introductory chapter, Debicki establishes why these poets form a generation. He also discusses the salient features, both thematic and stylistic, of the poetry of this generation of Spanish poets. Additional studies include José Luis Cano, *Poesía española contemporánea: generaciones de posguerra* (Madrid: Guadarrama, 1974); Jiménez, *Diez años de poesía española* 15-32; Jiménez, "Medio siglo de poesía española (1917-1967)," *Hispania* 50 (December 1967): 931-46, also "Poética y poesía de la joven generación española," *Hispania* 49 (May 1966): 195-205; and Philip W. Silver, "New Spanish Poetry: The Rodríguez-Brines Generation," *Books Abroad* 42 (1968): 211-14.

[4]Brines in Molina 528.

[5]Carlos Sahagún, "Notas sobre la poesía," in Francisco Ribes, *Poesía última* (Madrid: Taurus, 1963, 1969, 1975) 120.

[6]José Angel Valente, "Conocimiento y comunicación," in Ribes 157-58; also in Valente, *Las palabras de la tribu* (Madrid: Siglo XXI de España Editores, 1971) 7.

[7]One poem of *Aún no* is aptly titled "Métodos del conocimiento" (P 360).

[8] Hereafter, the poem titles, lines and page references from *Insistencias en Luzbel* (1977) will be given in the text.

[9]In my "Modes of Being in Francisco Brines' *Insistencias en Luzbel*," I show that Brines' ontological inquiry itself is a modification and original interpretation of the Heideggerian modes of authentic being (*eigentliche Existenz*) and unauthentic being (*uneigentliche Existenz*). See Martin Heidegger, *Sein und Zeit* (Halle, 1927), trans. J. Maquarrie and E.E. Robinson as *Being and Time* (New York: Harper and Row, 1962), where the German text is included marginally in the translation; also Werner Brock, "An Account of *Being and Time*," in *Existence and Being* (Chicago: Henry Regnery Co., 1949) analyzes, assesses and closely follows Heidegger's argument. Brock's insightful and highly regarded analysis is reproduced in *Reality, Man and Existence: Essential Works of Existentialism*, ed. H.J. Blackman (New York: Bantam Matrix Edition, 1956) 238-301. Hereafter Brock's study will be abbreviated ABT in these notes. Wolfgang Iser's notion of the "repertoire of a literary text" and its implications are applicable here. According to Iser, "The repertoire of a literary text does not consist solely of social and cultural norms; it also incorporates elements and, indeed, whole traditions of past literatures that are mixed together with these norms." In addition, literary allusions, like social and cultural norms, "open up familiar territory" and also "'quote' earlier answers to the problems – answers which no longer constitute a valid meaning for the present work, but which offer a form of orientation by means of which the new meaning may perhaps be found," *The Act of Reading. A Theory of Aesthetic Response* (Baltimore: The Johns Hopkins University Press, 1978) 79. One element among the many of the "repertoire" of Brines' *Insistencias en Luzbel* is the tradition of existential philosophy and literature. The allusions to, for example, Heidegger's philosophical investigations, and also those of other existentialists such as Jean-Paul Sartre and Sören Kierkegaard, to name but a few, are placed in a new context in *Insistencias en Luzbel* and within this new context they help to highlight important aspects of Brines' own ontological inquiry into and discovery of the meaning of Being.

[10]I use the term "human Being" in the Heideggerian sense of "human *Dasein*" or what could be called "human life," although, as Brock indicates, "both are not entirely the same" (ABT 240).

[11]See Brock, ABT 257-58, 266-75, for a discussion of the unauthentic mode of the self's "forgetfulness"of self-projection and becoming.

[12]See Debicki's observations regarding this poem (37-38) and also those of Persin (56-58).

[13]The voice of the poet/speaker is also heard in the following poems of *Insistencias en Luzbel*: "Invitación a un blanco mantel" (15), "Definición de la nada" (16), "Actos de supresión" (23-24), "Significación última" (29), "El oficio de servidor" (41), "Salvación en la oscuridad" (46), "Días finales" (81), and "El por qué de las palabras" (83-84). See Debicki's illuminating discussion of the theme of poetic creation and the role of the poet/speaker in *Insistencias en Luzbel* (37-38). The critic accurately observes: "The increasing stress on the theme of poetry in Brines's work, and the metapoetic nature of some of his recent texts, seem part of a general process of development. They constitute a way of moving beyond a 'realistic' presentation of his materials, of intensifying the play of perspectives, and of including the reader within a complex poetic inquiry into the theme of temporality. By commenting on the process of creation while undertaking it, the speaker invites us on the one hand to take part in it, and on the other to contemplate it as part of his general struggle against the order of things" (38). See also Persin's insightful chapter where she traces the poet's search for poetic expression in *Insistencias en Luzbel*.

[14]Iser indicates that "the interpreter's task should be to elucidate the potential meanings of a text, and not to restrict himself to just one. Obviously, the total potential can never be fulfilled in the reading process, but it is this very fact that makes it so essential that one should conceive of a meaning as something that happens, for only then can one become aware of those factors that precondition the composition of meaning" (*The Act of Reading* 22).

[15]See Iser's discussion of the reader's "ideational activity" (*The Act of Reading* 36, also 194-95 and 220-25).

[16]See Iser, *The Act of Reading* 34-36, 107-114, 163-70 and 180-231; also *The Implied Reader. Patterns of Communication in Prose Fiction from Bunyan to Beckett* (Baltimore: The Johns Hopkins University Press, 1974) 274-94.

[17]See *The Act of Reading* 38 and 107-14.

[18]Jean-Paul Sartre, *What is Literature?* trans. Bernard Frechtman (New York: Philosophical Library, 1949) 46. Contains the greater portion of *Situations II*.

[19]For a discussion of the concept of "dread" (*Angst*) see ABT 258-60.

[20]One is reminded of Sartre's observations: "For the word, which tears the writer of prose away from himself and throws him into the midst of the world, sends back to the poet his own image, like a mirror" (15).

[21]One aspect of the repertoire of this literary text is Sartre's notion of consciousness as a "vacancy," an "emptiness," a "gap between thought and the

object of thought" that Brines' image/metaphor of "el vacío" incorporates and modifies. See Mary Warnock, *The Philosophy of Jean-Paul Sartre* (London: Hutchinson University Library, 1965) 42-45 for a discussion of Part II of Sartre's *L'Être et le néant* (1943; *Being and Nothingness*) and "the gap within consciousness" (43).

[22]*The Implied Reader* xii. Iser defines the concept of the "implied reader" as follows: "The concept of the implied reader is . . . a textual structure anticipating the presence of a recipient without necessarily defining him: this concept pre-structures the role to be assumed by each recipient . . . The concept of the implied reader designates a network of response-inviting structures, which impel the reader to grasp the text" (*The Act of Reading* 34). Debicki investigates the textual structure of the implied reader, as defined by Iser, in Brines' poetry. See Chapter II of his study.

[23]For lack of a better term, I use the term "real" reader here to mean the actual reader of the poem: he/she who holds the book of poetry or the poem before him/her and is engaged in the act of reading. This real or actual reader is not linked to any historical period.

[24]For a discussion of the process of "filling in the gaps left by the text," see *The Implied Reader* 276-82; also see *The Act of Reading* 165-69. In addition, see "Indeterminacy and the Reader's Response in Prose Fiction," *Aspects of Narrative*, ed. J. Hillis Miller (New York; Columbia University Press, 1971) 1-45.

[25] *The Implied Reader* 280.

[26]Sartre 43.

[27]*The Implied Reader* 294.

[28]I would like to thank Dr. J. Christopher Maloney for discussing this essay with me. I would also like to thank the Committee on Faculty Research Support and Dean Robert Johnson, Graduate Studies and Research, of Florida State University for awarding me a research grant which made possible the investigation of Brines' poetry.

POESIA "CONCEPTUAL" EN ESPAÑA: LA PRODUCCION DE IGNACIO PRAT

Ignacio-Javier López
University of Virginia

> *La historia está en tiernas claves;*
> *vos ausente*
>
> Antonio Carvajal

El 16 de enero de 1982 fallecía en Barcelona Ignacio Prat a los 36 años de edad. Dejaba a su muerte libros de crítica sobre Jorge Guillén, el modernismo español, Blanco White, y una investigación inédita sobre Juan Ramón. A esto hay que añadir más de 50 artículos y estudios sobre diversos temas de literatura española, siendo especialmente notables los dedicados a la poesía española contemporánea, posteriormente recogidos en libro.[1] Finalmente, y ésta es la faceta menos conocida de su actividad, dejaba varios libros de poesía, algunos editados por él mismo, inéditos los más. Recopilados por sus amigos, han sido editados en 1983 por José Luis Jover con tel título *Para ti*.[2]

El desconocimiento de la labor poética de Prat no puede causar sorpresas, pues si en todas partes se lee poca poesía, como es sabido, una producción como la de Prat tiene pocas posibilidades de alcanzar siquiera una discreta circulación. El poeta mismo parece haberla escrito para un reducido círculo de lectores, aspecto destacado por Gimferrer cuando señala: «tendemos a creer que Ignacio Prat, deliberadamente, oscureció el ámbito irradiador de su palabra poética, la ciñó a coloquio con un número no ampliable de iniciados» (*El País* 29-I-1982). En este sentido, hay que notar que no se distribuyeron jamás los ejemplares de los libros de poesía impresos en vida del autor. Como si Prat quisiera establecer claramente el carácter de *coloquio* de los mismos, los obsequiaba a sus amigos y conocidos, la mayoría de ellos poetas o críticos de poesía.

Cuando al fin fueron editados por Jover, se hizo evidente la dificultad que existía para definirlos. Una opinión singularmente negativa respecto a esta poesía ha sido expuesta por García Martín, quien la considera oscilante «entre el galimatías y la broma erudita».[3] Con una perspectiva diferente, e intentando entender el porqué de dichos poemas, Luis Maristany subrayaba especialmente su provisionalidad, fiándose sin duda excesivamente de la apariencia de los textos, añadiendo que parecían «más apuntes que poemas propiamente dichos; materiales y divertimentos de su taller» (*La Vanguardia* 4-X-1983). Ana María Navales se acercaba a la poesía de Prat intentando determinar su efecto, hablando de «una turbina que la inteligencia aplica a la palabrería ... [y] que se apoya en el equívoco y prolonga el in-

genio» (*Heraldo de Aragón*; desconozco la fecha de esta reseña).
Por mi parte, creo que puede intentarse una definición puramente descriptiva e indicar que, primero, la producción de Prat es característicamente no mimética, pues no narra ni cuenta nada; y, segundo, su propósito es iniciar una reflexión sobre el arte como tal. En otras palabras, en la poesía de Prat el arte se orienta o dirige al arte mismo.

Partiendo de esta definición, mi propósito es adentrarme en esa reflexión propuesta en la producción de Prat y tratar de determinar posteriormente de qué modo tal reflexión se centra en la obra del grupo de poetas que Castellet denominó «coqueluche» y presentó en su afamada antología de 1970 con el título *Nueve novísimos poetas españoles*.

En principio, los rasgos descritos previamente hacen coincidir la poesía de Prat con ciertos experimentos poéticos que se desarrollan en los países occidentales durante la década de los 70, y que han recibido diferentes denominaciones. La variación de nombre suele implicar variación en el medio de trabajo y distinta orientación. Dos son sin duda sus denominaciones más comunes: poesía «concreta» y poesía «conceptual». A fin de llevar a cabo una distinción tajante entre ambas, con el fin de lograr mayor claridad expositiva, puede decirse que la poesía «concreta» trata de hacer inexpresable lo decible al crear una síntesis que impide la articulación verbal pero que, por contrapartida, logra la recuperación del objeto. A este respecto, en una definición reciente aparecida en la revista *Poesía*, Boso expresaba así la actividad de esta poesía: «En una ocasión propicia, sustituya un dormitorio por la palabra dormitorio; coloque en el interior de esta palabra la palabra lecho. Introdúzcase en la primera y extiéndase sobre la segunda. Tras un breve período de tiempo, duerma profundamente» (*Poesía*, 11, 117). En suma, lo que la humorística definición de Boso pretende captar es esa sustitución del texto que busca la poesía «concreta», ese intento de llegar a la realidad.

De modo diferente, la poesía «conceptual», y este es el caso de Prat, trata de escribir lo no decible, lo que queda preso en las aglomeraciones consonánticas, sirviendo como ejemplo extremo las aliteraciones gráficas del tipo *lc-c-U-Ulc-(Lc)-lt-tlc-c* con que finaliza *Así se hace las efes*; el juego fónico de un poema como «A Paulette Gabaudan»—«¡Gracias por no ser yo essos sesos que coje Sosia» (61); o las relaciones sintácticas insospechadas del tipo: «¿Hacer catleia?; ¡no!; ¡para los gamos!» («Boston» 63). Así, pues, mientras que la poesía «concreta» intenta llegar a una síntesis silenciosa que recupere el objeto, la poesía «conceptual» intenta pulsar más allá de los límites del lenguaje articulado y enunciar el silencio que limita o bordea lo que puede decirse. De este modo, a los ejemplos anteriores, el primero de los cuales muestra una indecible combinación consonántica, y los dos siguientes se acercan al «glíglico» de Cortázar, han de añadirse las combinaciones retóricas del tipo de

«La o sana dice da» («Don Saturno» 78) que Ana María Navales explica hábilmente como resultado combinatorio de la secuencia «la osa nada dice» (*Heraldo*, cit.).

La precisión anterior nos permite ampliar la discusión propuesta. En primer lugar, la reflexión sobre el arte y, más concretamente, sobre las implicaciones del concepto "arte" es notable ya en los primeros poemas de Prat. Conviene subrayar el hecho de que estos poemas aparecieron en revistas universitarias y, por consiguiente, que iban dirigidas a un público familiarizado con la producción artística y, a la par, menos reacio a aceptar el experimento. Estos poemas se caracterizan por la peculiar disposición gráfica del texto y, en especial, por la orientación escrita del mismo, llegando en ocasiones a tomar la forma de inscripciones murales (inscripción similar al cartel que fuera vehículo de expresión en la conflictiva universidad española de los 60 y 70), como ilustran la disposición del poema en una columna, el uso de mayúsculas y el «ampersand» en el siguiente texto:

& helleboro
& mi muñeca GIME
MI CORZAON GIME Y
estoy obsesionado por la nuez
del caballo de la nuez
en la actualidad me
deslizo por el deslizo
& hago incursiones obvias
en la P P de Noam Chomski
(«Help Auxilio» 103).

La orientación escrita del poema y su disposición espacial permiten establecer esa reflexión que se exige al lector y, al mismo tiempo, permiten la enunciación de los límites del poema. Así, por ejemplo, en «Se ha comparado la vida humana», de 1967, Prat escribe el poema a dos columnas, con una forma enumerativa que recuerda el formato del cartel e, incluso, las enumeraciones deductivas de los textos ensayísticos. Y dice:

Se ha comparado
la vida humana
... a Ovo novo no velho.
(«Se ha comparado ...» 104)

Quienes estén familiarizados con los experimentos de poesía «concreta» reconocerán fácilmente la composición OVONOVELO del poeta brasileño Augusto de Campos como núcleo del texto anterior. Sobre OVONOVELO, Décio Pignatari ha indicado que intenta objetualizar el poema-niño, la gestación biológica que en su forma recuperará la creación artística, la materialización misma del poema.

OVONOVELO es, por tanto, ese objeto-poema al que se llega mediante la adición y síntesis de OVO (huevo), NOVO (nuevo), VELO (vello, vello púbico), NOVELO (madeja, ovillo), NO VELHO (en lo viejo).⁴ Lo que Prat establece, al desmembrar dicha síntesis en sus componentes iniciales, es la secuencia escrita que subyace al ejemplo concreto. De este modo, se hace patente la orientación conceptual, escrita, que va a caracterizar a su poesía posterior.

En 1978 aparece *Así se hacen las efes*, volumen que parte de un verso de Juan Ramón («dulces luces azules de túneles y buques»), que fue objeto de una discusión teórica por parte del mismo Juan Ramón, la cual se recoge en la página 81 del libro de Gullón, *Conversaciones con JRJ*. Partiendo de este verso, que ya supone obviamente una codificación artística muy elaborada, el poema de Prat avanza en la reflexión conceptual investigando todas las posibilidades de su objeto, que es el arte, el poema mismo, como fuera dicho anteriormente. El procedimiento de investigación resulta ser una serie de derivaciones retóricas, de las que tiene especial interés la denominada palíndromo. Esta figura ha sido definida negativamente por Todorov, quien señala su carácter de «pur exercice de virtuosité. Acte gratuit par excellence, dépourvu de toute fonction« (apud EPC 93). Otros teóricos, sin embargo, han indicado su enorme carga potencial en la elaboración del texto artístico, y el mismo Prat registra su uso en Juan Ramón y Sábato, a los que pueden añadirse el Cabrera Infante de *Tres tristes tigres* y el Fuentes de *Terra Nostra*. La mayor potencialidad del palíndromo, sin embargo, está en su realización parcial, y Prat registra su uso en *Casi una fantasía* de Antonio Carvajal, en la conjunción de vocales que logra el magnífico verso «r̲o̲to̲s̲ l̲o̲s̲ l̲a̲zo̲s̲ pr̲o̲nt̲o̲ el alb̲o̲r̲o̲z̲o̲" (i.e., oooao/oaooo), o en las elaboraciones metafóricas del tipo «jó̲v̲e̲ne̲s»/«v̲e̲nce̲jos» (i.e., oee/eeo; vid. EPC 93 y 196-97).

En *Así se hacen las efes* el palíndromo es usado para reelaborar un objeto ya codificado artísticamente (el verso de Juan Ramón) y, mediante actos de virtuosismo, el poema alcanza una dimensión espacial con la adición de diagramas y la organización del poema, pues, al texto, generalmente una línea, sigue la página en blanco como espacio de reflexión. De este modo, y en función de la colaboración reflexiva del receptor, el poema va creciendo mediante sucesivas combinaciones: la combinación de los fonemas clave del verso juanramoniano (U, L, Ø, T) genera las combinaciones fundamentalmente consonánticas de la última parte del libro, antes citadas. Estas combinaciones pueden definirse como aliteraciones escritas que permiten llegar a lo desusado y enunciar aquello que no puede decirse porque no es articulable, pero que es expresable gracias a la movilidad dinámica del poema. Importa destacar que no se trata de una recuperación o vuelta al grito originario, vocálico, del tipo intentado por Huidobor en *Altazor*, sino que, de modo muy diferente, y para usar una metáfora derrideana, se intenta trazar, impulsar la escritura en un juego consonántico que permita llegar más allá del límite de lo decible, que permita, en suma, enunciar el silencio que bordea al poema. Finalmente, como muestra del trabajo que el texto artístico supone, el poema deja ver la tachadura, lo cual proporciona buena parte de su carga visual y evoca el otro silencio, el silencio de lo eliminado.[5] Enunciados de este modo los dos silencios que limitan y a la vez comparten el texto, se llega a lo que un teórico moderno consideraba la función de la nueva poesía: determinar la temperatura informacional del poema.

Pero ahora puede precisarse más esa temperatura informacional del poema. En *La muerte en Beverly Hills* (1968), último libro de poesía publicado por Gimferrer en castellano, el verso de Juan Ramón previamente citado es concebido como signo generacional o, parafraseando al mismo Gimferrer, como «sombra de mi juventud, en una usual figuración poética»; cabe añadir a esto que el verso es puesto como motivo inicial al frente del volumen en la primera edición, publicada por El Bardo.[6] En tanto que signo generacional, dicho verso es reelaborado en *La muerte* hasta el punto de ser la base sobre la que surgen los poemas del libro. La presencia del verso juanramoniano en el libro de Gimferrer es notable: «bajo el jersey *azul* / se para suave el corazón ... *dulces* hoces de hierro ... salvad mi corazón bajo la *luz* pesada!» (54); «aeropuertos de *luces azules*» (57); «*Luces* en un cristal ... en la *dulce* penumbra van y vienen, de la *azul* lejanía ... los albatros» (62). En suma, puede concluirse que Gimferrer intenta elaborar un lenguaje poético en *La muerte* mediante la reflexión sobre el verso citado de Juan Ramón, el cual es asumido como signo generacional.

Gimferrer ha sido considerado, junto con Carnero, uno de los poetas más destacables del grupo de poetas «Novísimos». Prat demostró siempre gran interés crítico por este grupo de poetas, a quienes se refirió todavía en una conferencia pronunciada un mes antes de su muerte (EPC 211-26). En ella indicaba lo siguiente: 1) que no existe ya tal generación, a pesar de los intentos editoriales por presentar a este grupo de poetas como la última generación de poetas peninsulares; 2) este grupo había dejado de existir antes de que apareciera la mencionada antología, pues Gimferrer, una de las figuras más notables del grupo, había dejado de escribir en castellano en 1969; y, 3) que algunos de los poetas incluidos en el grupo de la «coqueluche» pervivía imitando el lenguaje generacional de Gimferrer. Intentando reflexionar sobre la solución a los problemas planteados tras la separación de Gimferrer, Prat refería una fábula del siquiatra francés Emmanuel Régis y que puede resumirse del siguiente modo: un enfermo accedió a confesarse con su médico por escrito ya que no se atrevía a hacerlo oralmente; poco a poco fue considerando el idioma incapaz de expresar lo que él quería decir, llegando a entregar páginas llenas de tachaduras. Una vez que llegó a la página negra, completamente tachada, el paciente empezó por el principio, por el idioma corriente.

Este diagnóstico crítico de Prat sobre la poesía de los «Novísimos» nos permite ver una dimensión adicional de *Así se hacen las efes*, libro que se escribe cuatro años antes de la conferencia referida. El punto de partida es el verso de Juan Ramón, como se dijo, usado por Gimferrer como punto de partida de su lenguaje generacional. Las combinaciones virtuosas a que le somete Prat, previamente descritas, intentan reflexionar de un modo abstracto sobre el proceso creador, sobre la génesis del lenguaje y, finalmente, llegando a la tachadura final, el poema enuncia la página negra de la fábula anteriormente referida.

Sin embargo, lo que importa de esta nueva dimensión del poema es que, en principio, identifica al lector que sería, según lo expuesto, el poeta «novísimo» (llamémoslo así) y, segundo, que dicho poema reemplaza la actividad del crítico, pues el poema de Prat intenta crear en sí mismo la reflexión sobre el arte como tal. Este reemplazo es una característica fundamental de la poesía «conceptual», la cual intenta abolir la mediación crítica o, lo que es lo mismo, la crítica exterior al poema. Este deseo puede parecer paradójico en un crítico literario y profesor de literatura como Prat, de igual modo a como ocurre con otros poetas europeos, como Siegfried Joseph Schmidt, autor de varios libros de teoría y crítica literaria y, a la vez, poeta conceptual. Sin embargo, esta paradoja es tan sólo aparente si se atiende a los problemas planteados por la mediación crítica. En el capítulo VI de su *Foundations for the Empirical Study of Literature*, Schmidt ha detallado los distintos procesos de mediación literaria. Según él, toda obra artística exige, entre otras mediaciones de diverso tipo, la mediación crítica para ser entendida. Esta mediación supone, desde un punto de vista exclusivamente lingüístico, la decodificación del lenguaje específico de la obra de arte y la condificación mimética.[7] En otras palabras, el arte sufre un deterioro de su propia naturaleza como tal obra de arte. Por ello, el arte «conceptual», dirigido exclusivamente a especialistas, intenta evitar este deterioro al proponer la reflexión sobre el objeto de arte como tal. En este sentido, un poeta conceptual alemán, Kosruth, ha resumido de modo patente esta actitud al indicar:

> In its strictest and most radical extreme the art that I call conceptual is just that, because it is founded on an investigation of the nature of art. Thus it does not merely consist of the activity of producing statements on art, but of elaborating and thinking over all implications in every aspect of the notion "art." On account of the implicit duality of perception and content in former art, a mediator (critic) appeared to be

104

useful. This new art takes charge of the critic's function and thus no longer has any need for a mediator ... The audience of conceptual art consists mostly of artists.[8]

La reflexión previa nos permite recapitular ahora sobre lo expuesto anteriormente respecto a la poesía de Prat, y determinar la característica fundamental de su interés. En principio, es una poesía «conceptual» caracterizada por el intento de abolir, o al menos reemplazar, la labor crítica. El poema, por tanto, sustituye la mediación crítica e inicia una reflexión «desde dentro» del poema, usando un lenguaje que no es ajeno al arte. De ahí, por tanto, que el poema no sea mimético ni dé una narración, simplemente porque no es una labor crítica exterior al poema y porque toda explicación tiende a ser mimética y, por tanto, a convertir el objeto artístico en una narración, lo cual elimina elementos fundamentales de la naturaleza del poema.

Para entender lo que decimos quizá convenga que nos detengamos un instante en el siguiente poema del alemán Gomringer:[9]

schwiegen schwiegen schweigen	silencio silencio silencio
schweigen schweigen schweigen	silencio silencio silencio
schweigen schweigen	silencio silencio
schweigen schwiegen schweigen	silencio silencio silencio
schweigen schweigen schweigen	silencio silencio silencio

En sentido estricto, este poema «es» la escritura del silencio en, al menos, tres dimensiones (primero, el silencio que se produce entre una escritura y su traducción, aquí expresado entre dos columnas que no se comunican; segundo, el silencio literal, pues lo escrito es «silencio»; y, finalmente, el silencio del hueco central en tanto que espacio en blanco); y este poema «no es» la narración que yo he tenido que añadir entre paréntesis para explicarlo, haciendo uso de un orden sucesivo que rompe con la simultaneidad propia del poema, pues dicho paréntesis es una mediación crítica que viene impuesta por la necesidad de dar cuenta del texto y, además, por la necesidad de remitir su sentido a algo exterior (lo que menciona el uso de comillas en mi paréntesis explicativo, uso de comillas que, además, demuestra que yo, al usar lenguaje crítico, uso un lenguaje diferente al lenguaje propio del poema).

De este modo, cuando Prat escribe: «Así se hacen las efes»; y en la página siguiente añade «Como un elástico tropo expreso», lo escrito no es una explicación sino estrictamente una escritura que se extiende en una línea escasa, a la que sigue la página en blanco como espacio de reflexión. Partiendo de esta reflexión, se intenta llegar a establecer las implicaciones de la producción artística en cuanto a tal, pero siempre usando un lenguaje que al poema pertenece. Dicha reflexión parte de versos de otros autores y, en el caso particular de *Así se hacen las efes*, de un verso de Juan Ramón, previamente discutido teóricamente por el autor. Especial interés tiene en la elaboración de Prat la figura del «palíndromo», fundamentalmente por el virtuosismo que implica y porque dicho virtuosismo, hecho casi gratuito según Todorov, no tiene otra justificación que la del poema mismo; no tiene, por tanto, más sentido que el de mostrar la elaboración que el poema supone, elaboración que especifican los diagramas mismos, que además sirven para invitar al lector a continuar los juegos de virtuosismo que en el texto se trazan – Cf.:

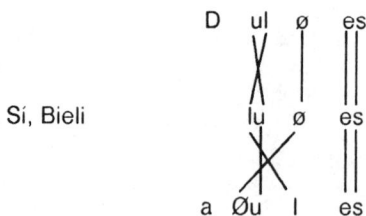

D   ul   ø   es

Sí, Bieli   lu   ø   es

a   Øu   l   es

Finalmente, mediante derivaciones retóricas, el poema de Prat manifiesta a través de la escritura todas las dimensiones del texto, enunciando incluso los dos silencios, lo no articulable y lo tachado, como límites y complementos del poema. El resultado es la escritura de lo inarticulable, la tachadura:

DE - MI

Lc-c-U-Ulc-(Lc)-lt-tlc-c-(XXXXXXX)-Ult-tls-
ls-Lcs-Uls-Us-l-clU-ctU-stc-Lc-cU-c-cU-U-U-U-
ctlsc-t(m-que-á)-litro)-sc-s-s-lts.

Pero han de tenerse en cuenta dos hechos importantes: primero, que la escritura de lo inarticulable está formada por elementos procedentes de la combinación de los sonidos fundamentales del verso juanramoniano; y, segundo, que la tachadura (representada en el texto con X) aparece como difuminación del «yo» en la combinación *demi de mí* (mitad de mí mismo) a que aluden las mayúsculas del texto.[10]

Por otra parte, en tanto que reflexión sobre el arte, el poema de Prat identifica a su receptor: el poeta «novísimo», que viene determinado por la reelaboración del verso juanramoniano mencionado, usado por Gimferrer como signo generacional, como punto de partida para crear un lenguaje poético. Considerado el desenlace del grupo de los «Novísimos» a partir de 1969, por la separación de Gimferrer, y la pervivencia de este poeta en la creación de algunos de los miembros del grupo, el poema de Prat supone una invitación a la reflexión sobre la creación poética, invitación que, en las combinaciones que muestra en su propia derivación, reproduce el proceso de creación original del mismo Gimferrer.

NOTAS

[1]I. Prat, *Estudios sobre poesía contemporánea* (Madrid: Taurus, 1982); en adelante EPC, y se indica la página entre paréntesis.

[2]I. Prat, *para ti, 1963-1981* (Valencia: Pre-Textos, 1983).

[3]J.L. García Martín, *Poesía española 1982-1983* (Madrid: Hiperión, 1983) 99.

[4]D. Pignatari, «Concrete Poetry», *Poetics Today* 3.3 (1982): 191.

[5]P.ej., la tachadura es la base de la composición «Cancellatura» de Emilio Isgró en la muestra de *poesía visiva* de Eugenio Micini, *Poesia y/o poesia* (Brescia: SRMICR, 1972), s/p. Un ejemplo adicional de este tipo de cancelación o tachadura, a cargo esta vez de un poeta español, puede verse reproducido en S. Sanz Villanueva, *Historia de la litratura española: Literatura actual* (Barcelona: Ariel, 1984) 459.

[6]Todas las citas, sin embargo, proceden de la edición de *Poemas 1963-1969* (Madrid: Visor, 1979). El énfasis es siempre mío.

[7]S.J. Schmidt, *Foundations for the Empirical Study of Literature* (Amsterdam: H. Buske, 1982) 124-33.

[8]Kosruth, apud S.J. Schmidt, «Perspectives on the Development of Post-Concrete Poetry», *Poetics Today* 3.3 (1982): 114.

[9]Apud Liselotte Gumpel, *«Concrete» Poetry from East and West Germany* (New Haven: Yale University Press, 1976). Alejandro Amusco, «Ignacio Prat, el sueño tardío del cubismo», *El País* 23-11-1982, ya ha señalado la conexión posible de Prat con la poesía alemana, en particular con Gappmayr; el ideograma «Sind» de Gappmayr, recogido en la página 198 del ilbro citado de Gumpel, serviría para sustentar la afirmación del poeta y crítico sevillano.

[10]Sobre esta escritura del «yo», vid. mi «Ignacio Prat o el poema en activo», *Hora de poesía* 23-24 (1982): 91-98.

PURIFICACION Y ESENCIALIDAD EN LA MAS JOVEN POESIA

Biruté Ciplijauskaité
University of Wisconsin-Madison

Proponerse señalar ciertos rumbos en la evolución de la poesía reciente en una exposición relativamente breve lleva siempre el riesgo de repetir lugares comunes sin añadir nada nuevo. Por otra parte, enfocar sólo una de las direcciones tiende a oscurecer la visión global. El presente trabajo se presenta a sabiendas como un intento de acercamiento a un solo sector de la poesía de los últimos años. La elección de tal enfoque ha sido motivada por el reciente fallecimiento de Jorge Guillén: en vez de intentar una visión panorámica, el estudio se ofrece como un homenaje a Guillén, proponiéndose destacar algunos libros de poesía más recientes donde se pueda percibir cierta afinidad (de actitud, de tono, de hechura del verso) con el poeta desaparecido. Para no reducir del todo la visión, se intentará presentar muy brevemente la situación general, apuntando las corrientes prevalecientes, precisar luego algunas diferencias entre éstas y la herencia guilleniana, y proceder por fin a estudiar con más pormenor lo que une la obra de cuatro poetas jóvenes (María Victoria Atencia, Alejandro Amusco, Jaime Siles, Luis Suñén) con la de Guillén. El procedimiento no será estrictamente histórico; esto permitirá no entrar en deliberaciones sobre lo que representa una «generación» o una «promoción», que ha suscitado tantas polémicas últimamente.[1]

Al tratar de descubrir afinidades entre Jorge Guillén y los jóvenes poetas, habrá que escuchar ante todo las voces más personales y conscientes, con menos tendencias de grupo. Se destacará sobre todo a aquellas para las cuales la poesía representa su razón de ser, no principalmente juego, experimentación o algo inútil.[2] Douglass Rogers ha señalado el proceso de la desmitificación de la palabra desde Aleixandre — «No, no quedan los nombres» —,[3] pasando por José Hierro — «Y lo demás, palabras, palabras y palabras» —,[4] hasta los representatantes más jóvenes.[5] A su vez, María Nowakowska Stycos ha mostrado cómo el escepticismo trae como amenaza una evolución hacia el silencio en Brines.[6] Los poetas escogidos para ser considerados por sus posibles correspondencias con Guillén manifiestan fe en la palabra, creencia en el «conjunto» estructurado («La forma se me vuelve salvavidas» afirmaba Guillén en «Hacia el poema»):

> Me remueve tu voz. Por ella siento
> que la rama combada se endereza
> y el fruto de mi voz se crece al viento[7]

una fe que en algun caso determina su actitud ya no sólo frente a la poesía, sino también frente a la vida.

Las antologías de la «joven poesía» han ido surgiendo con profusión poco habitual en los últimos diez o quince años. No por eso resulta más fácil orientarse en el panorama poético actual: cada editor aplica criterios muy personales que tiñen también las introducciones.[8] Hablar hoy de los «novísimos» parece ya casi anticuado. Sin embargo, en las consideraciones que siguen habrá que referirse a este grupo de poetas, ya que al principiar la década de los setenta fijaron ciertos rumbos y contribuyeron a la formación de una voz diferente.

La presencia de Jorge Guillén es menos palpable entre los jóvenes poetas que la de Aleixandre, Cernuda,[9] Octavio Paz o Paul Celan. En la introducción a su *Joven poesía española*, Rosa María Pereda señala que la influencia de Guillén llega relativamente tarde e indirectamente: a través de José Angel Valente (15). En un artículo anterior, simplificando la situación, sugería: «Creo que ahora se puede decir ya que hay dos líneas maestras para la poesía joven española que vienen del grupo del 27: la que parte de Aleixandre y la que encuentra su magisterio en Jorge Guillén».[10] Constatación cuyo origen se podría buscar en el número 1 de *Poesía*, donde aparecen yuxtapuestos textos de los dos autores documentando la divergencia de rumbo. Mientras que Aleixandre sugiere que «cuando nace un poeta lo que nace es un silencio» (6), Guillén sigue en sus trece, afirmando inequívocamente la plenitud y añadiendo una pregunta que parece dirigirse a los críticos que le han reprochado su «máscara de perfección»:

Esa final efusión
Portadora de la vida
Nos muda en centro radiante
De plenitud conseguida.

¿Condenas el vivir desde ese centro?[11]

Es de notar que este mismo número incluye también, en presentación bilingüe, varios poemas de Paul Celan, traducidos por José Angel Valente, de los cuales retenemos un verso: «ein ins Stumme entglittenes Ich» (40). Referencias a esta mudez, al lenguaje como prisión («Sprachgitter») se harán cada vez más frecuentes entre los jóvenes poetas en la última década.

El impacto de Aleixandre parece un fenómeno natural: es la grande figura patriarcal de la poesía española desde los primeros años de posguerra. Su persona, su presencia, el contacto personal, la actitud siempre alentadora no pueden no dejar huella en los poetas incipientes. A esto hay que añadir la fascinación de las múltiples facetas de su poesía: una obra en constante evolución, más fácilmente identificable con el contexto en el que viven. La liberación de versículo, las avalanchas de palabras, las desbordantes estructuras telúricas o cosmogónicas de sus primeros libros ofrecen gran variedad de aspectos y técnicas en que inspirarse. A su vez, el escepticismo cada vez más acentuado de los últimos coincide con la cosmovisión de cierto sector del mundo moderno más fácilmente que la «alegría conquistada» de Guillén. Este escepticismo encamina al poeta a la ambigüedad del monólogo que parece anunciar un enmudecer completo, que tiene puntos de contacto con la postura de Celan en el verso citado.[12]

Jorge Guillén ha vuelto a establecerse en España sólo en los años setenta, y en Málaga. Su radio no podía alcanzar a tantos. No hay violenta desesperación ni escepticismo de base en su obra. La dificultad de seguir su ejemplo estriba no sólo en el rigor formal de su poesía o la exactitud de su palabra: mucho más difícil de asumir es su actitud afirmativa, su fe, aceptación, exaltación de la vida. Actitud denunciada por algunos como artificial, pero que ha persistido con una continuidad extraordinaria, tanto en su obra como en su vida. La poesía de Guillén no separa estética de la ética. Su crear es la elaboración de un ideal de vida, lo que Ortega llamaba el proyecto vital: «yo soy mi cotidiana tentativa».[13] El acto creador no representa para él meramente una aventura lingüística: es una constante vital. De aquí su crítica de la irresponsabilidad frente a la palabra, de metáforas gratuitas que sólo buscan deslumbrar, de juegos puramente técnicos.

Parece lícito aducir también un factor biográfico en el intento de precisar las diferencias: Jorge Guillén empieza a escribir poesía a los 25 años y publica su primer libro cuando tiene 35: una edad en la que su voz y su cosmovisión están firmemente establecidas. Hoy algunos poetas ofrecen ya sus «Obras completas» apenas llegando a los 30: la poesía en castellano de Pere Gimferrer; la producción poética de Guillermo Carnero; la poesía reunida de Jaime Siles. Es como si se prepararan para un cambio. Lo resume irónicamente Luis Alberto de Cuenca: «Antes de cumplir treinta años hemos muerto».[14] La evolución es hoy más rápida y radical, como lo demuestra la obra de un Siles o de un Suñén.

Jorge Guillén empieza desde el primer momento con una voz personal, inconfundible.[15] En muchos de los jóvenes se percibe primero lo que se podría llamar la voz y la actitud de su tiempo o del grupo, que ha recibido varias denominaciones por parte de los críticos: marginalidad, culturalismo, venecianismo. Esta voz era necesaria para marcar una ruptura. En la evolución ulterior de cada uno de estos poetas resulta más difícil encasillarla bajo un rótulo, porque se ha vuelto mucho más personal y original. Si Guillén ofrece su esencia desde el principio, los jóvenes evolucionan hacia las esencias sobre todo en los últimos años.

Los títulos de Guillén indican que él canta siempre en plena voz: *Cántico, Clamor*. Entre los jóvenes, sólo *Hymnica* de Luis Antonio de Villena ofrece una sugerencia semejante, matizando a la vez su procedencia culta. En este libro se presenta una Belleza ideal, anhelada, fabulada y a la vez puesta en duda. La voz no alcanza plena fuerza de persuasión, no es sostenida por una vivencia inmediata. Por otra parte, ya se ha hecho alusión a la evolución que representa la obra de un sector entero de los jóvenes (el último José Angel Valente, Pere Gimferrer de *Apariciones*, Jaimes Siles en *Música de agua*): se encaminan hacia lo que Amparo Amorós ha llamado muy certeramente «la retórica del silencio».[16]

Para Jorge Guillén la palabra poética es una parte integral y la coronación de la experiencia vital: «Si del todo vivir, decir del todo» («Vida extrema»). Para ciertos jóvenes es ante todo instrumento o tema. Pere Gimferrer señala que el cambio ha ocurrido ya en los primeros años de la posguerra, y que los jóvenes de su generación echaban de menos un «puente» entre el gran grupo del 27 y sus propios contemporáneos: un puente que en su caso particular encontró en Octavio Paz: «La poesía de Paz encarnaba como pocas aquello que, en el momento presente, podía justificar aún la existencia misma de la poesía como género literario. Hablo de una doble justificación: estética y moral. Hablo, pues, de una *razón de ser*.[17] Más arriba se ha aludido al escepticismo creciente hacia la palabra por parte de representantes de varias generaciones, que va aumentando entre los jóvenes. Frente a ello, Guillén no ceja: — «'Words, words, words.' — No. Palabras prodigiosas.»[18] Mientras que entre los jóvenes resurge la admiración por Wallace Stevens, quien examina casi ontológicamente la palabra, Jorge Guillén, cuya obra tiene alguna afinidad con la de éste, insiste en el poder de la palabra sobre la vida, basado en la vida misma.

Esta es otra divergencia notable entre Jorge Guillén y ciertos jóvenes: su actitud frente a la realidad. Desde «Más allá» el autor de *Aire nuestro* ha repetido: «La realidad me inventa, / Soy su leyenda.» En los novísimos se puede observar un alejamiento consciente de ella, cuyas raíces hay que buscar en su reacción contra la «poesía social». Lo ha mostrado persuasivamente A. Debicki al analizar un poema muy reciente de Amparo Amorós.[19] Durante la década de los setenta frecuentemente parten del arte y de la literatura: Bousoño señala en ellos una base de ficción (26). L.A. de Cuenca habla de «reescritura» como «nuestro acto de crear» (247). Por otra parte, algunos, como Ignacio Prat en «La página negra» o Jaime Siles en su «Poética», insisten en la necesidad de recuperar la realidad, cada uno a su modo. Incluso en los aspectos negativos cabe distinguir matices: los jóvenes hacen hincapie en la paradoja que ofrece la realidad; Guillén siempre está dispuesto a tratar de enderezarla. El concepto mismo de la poesía no es el mismo. Jorge Guillén la ve como un quehacer ininterrumpido, un «conjunto» que traduzca su «fe de vida». Este concepto de la Obra hoy día parece haber caído en desuso. Basta hojear un par de antologías para tropezar con declaraciones que afirman todo lo contrario: «Más que la poesía — y su profesionalidad — me interesa el texto poético como realización de una aventura lingüística que transparente el proceso de transcripción de nuestra percepción de la realidad. Y porque cada poema es un universo autónomo, tendríamos que detenernos en el análisis de sus poéticas posibles«, afirma Eugenio Padorno.[20] Jaime Gil de Biedma lo dice casi con las mismas palabras: «y la poesía, mejor dicho, los poemas — yo pienso más en términos de poemas que en términos de poesía — son cosas creadas, artefactos».[21] Se impone la fragmentación.

El que los poetas jóvenes no busquen una Obra total no significa, sin embargo, que no les interese el aspecto formal-estructural. Todo lo contrario: su poesía nace como protesta contra el arbitrario prosaísmo y «liberalidad» de algunos poetas de los años 50-60. La arquitectura les fascina tanto como a Jorge Guillén. Sólo el matiz es diferente. En Jorge Guillén la figura principal es el círculo que significa la plenitud. Los jóvenes construyen desde la memoria cultural y a causa de su actitud vital se acercan no pocas veces a lo que Jaime Siles, al analizar unos poemas de Góngora, ha denominado «la arquitectura del desengaño».[22] No parece una exageración sugerir que les es aplicable también la observación de Siles acerca de los procedimientos de Góngora que surgen de su actitud general: de tener más fe en el mito que en la circunstancia inmediata (95). Se crea una realidad que depende del sistema de referencias míticas (mitos modernos en el caso de los jóvenes). Mientras que los versos de Guillén atestiguan una fe renovada con cada contacto real, que le llena de gozo, los jóvenes construyen sobre contactos de segundo grado. La palabra, entonces, según señala Siles, «ya no puede ser reflejo, sino salvación de la realidad» (149). Perdidos la fe o el interés en la realidad inmediata, la palabra es lo único que queda. Julia Barella hace observar que para los jóvenes el lenguaje parece ser «la única posibilidad de ordenación. ... El lenguaje se mitifica y así ejerce su autoridad sobre el propio poeta que se convierte en siervo de la ficción o del artificio en el que él mismo ha participado».[23] En más de una ocasión tales estructuras dejan percibir la nada como trasfondo. Lo ha notado Barella: «La revelación del vacío y del azar — el anticausalismo — hace inaprehensible o fútil lo existente. Vacío real, vacío verbal o imagen que resulta de dos espejos enfocados».

La presencia o ausencia de la fe que permite concebir el mundo como armonía matiza la formulación de las relaciones entre las partes constituyentes del universo. Entre los jóvenes la tensión entre «unicidad y dualidad, o pluralidad», que Lucie Personneaux señala como una de las claves del mundo poético de Aleixandre, lleva a establecer un principio de intercambiabilidad.[24] Todo es plural y uno: «Todo es materia: tiempo, / espacio; carne y obra». Para Guillén, la materia no es una, ni intercambiable; sí anhelante de integrarse en el todo para asumir pleno significado: «Gozosa materia en relación» («Más allá»). Cada cosa tiene su perfil distinto, pero converge al final para ofrecer una estructura de plenitud: proceso puesto en evidencia en los versos finales de «Plaza Mayor»: «De pronto, cuatro son uno. / Victoria: bella unidad».

Todos los matices de la joven poesía aducidos hasta aquí se refieren sobre todo al primer lustro de los años 70. Hoy está ocurriendo un cambio, una ramificación. Lo que ha servido como punto de partida ha sido superado en más de un caso. La actitud prevaleciente al principio ha sido medio irónicamente resumida por Luis Alberto de Cuenca en 1979, usando en su descripción exclusivamente tiempos verbales pasados: «Si de algo hemos huído ha sido de la profesionalidad, de la responsabilidad ... Nos distraíamos y huíamos de las cosas en silencio y melancolía» (246). «Entendíamos la poesía ... momentánea y circunstancial, festiva, intrascendente, divertida e inútil» (250). La orientación de los últimos años señala direcciones nuevas: en algunos, hacia la filosofía; en otros, hacia la teoría del lenguaje. Se está prestando más atención a la composición. En ciertos casos, se le devuelve trascendencia a la palabra. Manuel Ríos Ruiz, intentando una visión panorámica, habla de un nuevo vitalismo entre los más jóvenes (Carlos Faraco, María Eugenia Salaverri, Rafael Cruz), que vuelven a lo cotidiano real y a la relación íntima con las cosas.[26] Van surgiendo poetas como Julio Llamazares (premio Jorge Guillén) o Andrés Trapiello, que poco tienen que ver con las modas. Tal vez sea demasiado pronto para afirmar rotundamente que ha tomado lugar un cambio radical. Una cosa no deja lugar a dudas: ha cambiado la situación. Hoy los poetas no tienen ya contra qué exhibir su actitud «anti-establishment». Ha desaparecido la causa exterior de sus protestas. Se reconoce que ha llegado la hora de construir, y se busca una voz completamente original.

Queda por ver si la nueva evolución eliminará una última diferencia que se podría señalar entre los principios de los poetas nuevos y Jorge Guillén. En Guillén la poesía surge del gozo de lo que se tiene, que dicta una actitud a la vez generosa y humilde. Así, cuando se asoma a la obra de otros, a pruebas del ingenio humano, lo hace como homenaje. La poesía de varios representantes de las generaciones sucesivas está basada en el deseo. Incluso el tema artístico no es siempre debido al contacto inmediato y se manifiesta como esto: tema. Así nace el culturalismo. La fe de Jorge Guillén lleva a la plenitud, y a través de ella a la reverencia. El escepticismo de los jóvenes a veces les hace asumir posturas arrogantes que en realidad encubren inseguridad. Con la madurez, van apareciendo notas más claras, palabras más esenciales. Persiste una curiosa diferencia: en Guillén, el énfasis en lo esencial se ha traducido por crecimiento constante, hasta que *Cántico* haya llegado a su plenitud final, a los 10,000 versos. Entre los jóvenes que llaman más la atención, el proceso parece haberse invertido. Al reunir sus cinco primeros libros en un volumen, declara Siles: «Toda obra es, necesariamente, supresión. Y, también, negación. ... 51 poemas en once años parecen demasiados.»[27] La línea ascendiente de *Cántico* se quiebra y va bajando hacia el silencio.

* * *

Después de la larga introducción, en la que se ha intentado indicar algunas diferencias, es hora ya de aventurarse a buscar afinidades. Como se ha señalado al principio, la admiración por Jorge Guillén ha ido creciendo, aunque su nombre no parezca en la «Poética» de los jóvenes con tanta frecuencia como el de Aleixandre, Cernuda, Celan, Kavafis. Una rápida ojeada a través de algunas antologías y libros aparecidos en los últimos años no deja duda, sin embargo, sobre su presencia. Así, en la encuesta sobre la poesía incluída como apéndice en *Una promoción desheredada*, —declaraba Mariano Roldán ya en 1978: «Guillén, poeta esencial —del que alguna vez declaré influencia—, claro que tiene que ver conmigo, y contigo, y con todo el que escriba verso español tras él y no sea adicto a los Juegos Florales».[28] En esta misma antología señalaba Carlos Barral más generalmente «una consciente voluntad de reanudar con la poética del 27» (313). Su admiración por Guillén encuentra expresión en «Guilleniana»: *Cántico* es el poemario, el libro unitario de poesía, más importante de los que se han escrito durante el siglo veinte en lengua castellana».[29] Angel González le ofrece un homenaje en *Prosemas o menos* (1983), Clara Janés en *Vivir* (1983), Martínez Sarrión en *Horizonte desde la rada* (1983). María Victoria Atencia le dedica un libro entero, *El coleccionista* (1979). Y en su sugeridor ensayo «Jorge Guillén: simetría y sistema», originalmente de 1976, Jaime Siles le presenta como «el más europeo de los poetas españoles de este siglo» y «ejemplo máximo de una de las formas más válidas en que la materia poética puede objetivarse».[30] Varios críticos han observado que él mismo, quien con tanta perspicacia ha analizado la obra guilleniana, asimila más de un procedimiento de éste.

La admiración que los poetas profesan a una grande figura no necesariamente significa que van a seguirle. Le han homenajeado poetas tan diferentes como Ignacio Prat, cuyo estudio sobre *Aire nuestro* permanece uno de los más serios y sugeridores que existan, y Antonio Carvajal. Algunos han concentrado su atención en la obra de Guillén como herencia, asimilando algún procedimiento o su actitud básica. En otros aparece como un destello suelto. Como tal podría considerarse el caso de Antonio Carvajal, en su totalidad muy diferente de la concisión guilleniana. Su *Tigres en el jardín* (1968) incluye algún poema que parece contener ecos de Jorge Guillén, como «Naturaleza ofrecida»: «Todo vive en la luz y la luz vive en todo, / y todo es una sola naturaleza acorde».[31] En *Sol que se alude* consta «Trébol», sugerente ya por el título, donde la inspiración aparece como forma y recuerda las variaciones de Guillén sobre la obra de otros poetas en *Homenaje*. J.L. García Martín cree percibir ecos guillenianos en la última parte de *Apariciones* de Pere Gimferrer y subraya la afirmación en algún verso de Clara Janés. Jaime Siles ha visto bien el complejo problema de las afinidades al comentar ciertos parecidos entre Claudio Rodríguez y Pedro Salinas: «Pero eso — y no otra cosa — es, en literatura, la singularidad: la forma en que el escritor se apropia y se hace digno de su herencia».[32] En lo que sigue intentaremos ver algunas de estas apropiaciones en la obra de cuatro poetas dispares, que no forman grupo ninguno, pero coinciden en adoptar ciertos procesos de purificación con la meta de llegar a la esencialidad.

*   *   *

La voz de María Victoria Atencia, la menos «novísima» de ellos, cuyo primer libro aparece ya en 1961, se afirma en realidad en *Marta María* (1976), cuyo título realza la dualidad latente en su obra, y más aún en *El mundo de M.V.* (1978). Ella nunca ha seguido modas, sino que ha ido edificando un mundo muy personal. No se ha permitido caer en la facilidad o la extravagancia. En una de sus últimas publicaciones mantiene que «el arte es amable y exigente».[33] Lo que más la acerca a Jorge Guillén es la aceptación de la realidad cotidiana y la valoración del íntimo gozo que emana de ésta. Su *El coleccionista* no sólo es dedicado a Jorgen Guillén: contiene un «proema» de Guillén que enumera las cualidades de la autora: «En ese verso noble y tan sencillo / Porque es noble, / Ya alzado hasta un extremo / De firme poesía . . . / generosa / Con la serenidad que es una gracia». El íntimo trato con el poeta desde que éste se estableciera en Málaga ha dejado sus huellas. En *El mundo . . .* se eleva lo cotidiano a lo esencial, se detiene el tiempo de los relojes sin dejar de poner de relieve la conciencia temporal (la palabra inicial del título de cada parte es «Tiempo»). Se ofrece el gozo del aquí y el ahora sin renunciar a cierta ilusión del mundo mágico. La complementación de las dos facetas es subrayada por la estructura (en esto, en la maestría formal, en el gusto por estructuras acabadas, reside otra afinidad con el maestro). En *El mundo . . .* todos los poemas consisten de dos partes: la realidad vivida y la soñada como partes iguales que no se estorban. Cada poema consta de dos estrofas de seis alejandrinos. La integración de ambas caras de la existencia humana le permite decir:

> Me asomo a las umbrías de cuanto en esta hora
> dispongo y pueda darme su reposo. (13)

o presentar como síntesis de esta coexistencia un verso que puede parecer paradójico: «Andar es no moverse del lugar que escogimos» (44): contraposición total al anhelo de evasión de algunos jóvenes. En su poesía no caben deseos insatisfechos ni grandes tensiones; sí hay diversidad, pero en equilibrio. El tono y la andadura pausados son característicos de este libro. Significan un universo aceptable y aceptado, donde el ahora y la eternidad se compaginan sin esfuerzo: «Dame la cámara / lenta en que pueda verme con mis cosas en torno» (15).

Como consecuencia de esta actitud básicamente afirmativa incluso lo que se podría llamar «culturalismo» se convierte en homenaje reminiscente del de Guillén. Cuando sale del mundo de las cosas cotidianas que la rodean, no va hacia referencias míticas o literarias, no formula anhelos apasionados. Más bien, así como Jorge Guillén, ofrece constataciones-variaciones acerca del lugar, cuadro, libro disfrutado. La cultura entra a través de la vivencia. En *El coleccionista* estos gozos se expresan en forma más abreviada, estrofas tenues que inmovilizan un instante. Con sus procedimientos logra una eternización de varios grados: lo que ha conservado el tiempo es fijado por la memoria inmediata y finalmente salvado por la palabra. Algunos de estos poemas se presentan casi en forma de «tréboles», construidos sobre un solo pensamiento, una sola intuición. No hay narración en ellos: sólo ordenación de las esencias. Son poemas ricos en imágenes, pero nunca efectistas; presentan experiencia objetivada, pero personal; la palabra exacta—«Y no falte a mi encanto la palabra precisa« (*Marta María*)—se inserta en una estructura siempre adecuada. Clara Janés ha resumido certeramente la disposición afirmativa de este libro: «consciente de la ruina, ofrece el arte; consciente de la fugacidad, el ahora, el instante; consciente del marchitarse, la plenitud; consciente de la crisis racionalista, la certeza; consciente de la muerte, la belleza».[34]

La parte central de *El coleccionista* refiere directamente a Jorge Guillén: «Cántico», «Huerto de Melibea»; aparecen afirmaciones como «su plenitud se cumple»; casi todo se desarrolla en el presente. El último poema, «Afán», recalca el «diario quehacer». El título del libro más reciente, *Adviento* (1983), con su connotación litúrgica que anuncia júbilo, indica que no ha renunciado a su postura básica. María Victoria Atencia se destaca entre sus contemporáneos por este aplomo sereno, por el gozo que para ella representa el vivir y moldear este vivir en palabras. Tiene fe en la palabra, y le deja el tiempo necesario para madurar. Entonces, se desprende como una fruta, pero en vez de caer, inicia una subida por el aire.

* * *

También Alejandro Amusco crea fuera de grupos. Su obra interesa por su evolución constante. Desde 1976 ha ido ensayando varios procedimientos, destacándose siempre por el verso cuidado y la maestría formal. También él parece tener fe en la palabra y en la capacidad del poeta de moldearla. Ya desde el primer libro busca lo esencial. A través de su obra es patente la relación con Aleixandre (hay que recordar asimismo sus ensayos de crítica literaria), pero en los poemas «esenciales» es evidente también la lección de Guillén, a quien en ocasión ha dedicado poemas. Amusco empieza con una voz sorprendentemente madura, que no se queja ni protesta contra nada. Los primeros dos libros se abren con la luz del amanecer, bajo la cual «se dispone el mundo». Este disponer es ayudado por la maestría del verso. El amor se integra con la naturaleza, como en los grandes poemas amorosos de *Cántico*, y los dos se vuelven afirmación contra el tiempo.

La estructura de su primer libro, *Esencias de los días* (1976), hace pensar en las tres partes de *Aire nuestro*: «Esencias de la luz», «Esencias de la sombra», «Esencias». Ya la progresión de los títulos revela deseo de síntesis — y de abreviación. Muchos elementos del primer libro tienen afinidad con la poesía guilleniana: títulos como «Fervor», afirmaciones jubilosas como «La vida así es hermosa» (21; nótese, sin embargo, la cuidadosa matización, ausente en Jorge Guillén: «así»). La sencilla constatación «Mi pasado es la esencia de mi nombre» (22) hace pensar en el guilleniano «Mi labor, mi ambición son en resumen: / Identidad personal en conjunto».[35] Este libro revela la «conquistada presencia» día a día y termina con luz que «enciende signos / en decisiva constelación de haces», bajo los cuales «Nazco. Escintilo. Sueno. ... Y amanezco» (54). Su poesía es una poesía ante todo nominal en esta colección, y muy consciente de lo que se puede conseguir a través de la estructura. Usa muy sabiamente las inversiones e intenta una síntesis o a veces una sorpresa en el último verso, con frecuencia separado tipográficamente.

El sol en Sagitario representa su fase experimental: más interés por imágenes y efectos sueltos, versículo desbordante, partes más narrativas, presencia del «yo» que a veces lleva casi al borde de lo sentimental. No está todo subordinado a una arquitectura total. No consigue objetivar siempre, pero ya aquí aparecen algunas estampas de puras esencias que anuncian la concisión de las partes centrales del volumen siguiente. En este libro se nota más afinidad con Aleixandre; penetran palabras como «gélido». La afirmación no ha

118

desaparecido, aunque no es tan constante: «El paraíso / no es artificial» (79). Como en *Esencias*, el último poema reanuda con el primero, poniendo de relieve luz y afirmación: «En algún sitio, lejos, la plenitud de una alondra. / Las campanas del amanecer» (95).

En *Del agua, del fuego y otras purificaciones* (1983), públicamente presentado por Carlos Bousoño en Madrid el 27 de marzo 1984, Amusco desarrolla más sus técnicas más características: la depuración de la estampa, la concentración de las esencias en el último verso del poema. Es un libro desigual, con partes que Siles denominaría «arborescencia metafórica», con algún regusto casi mítico. Por otra parte, este libro representa el madurar de la conciencia poética y énfasis en su significación, el tránsito casi palpable de lo dado a lo conseguido, de la palabra a la significación. La tarea de eternizar las esencias se enuncia como tema en la primera parte y es llevada a cabo en la tercera, en las *tannkas* que en realidad constan sólo de esencias depuradas: poemitas brevísimos que consisten en cinco versos a través de los cuales se distribuyen 31 sílabas, inspirados en la tradición oriental. En los poemas más logrados de las otras partes también llaman la atención la abreviación, la casi total ausencia del verbo, la colocación estratégica de las palabras que adquieren polivalencia y llegan a ser «esplendores ocultos» que se revelan en un «desgarramiento» repentino. Los efectos se consiguen a base de elipsis o variando una sola partícula. Véase como ejemplo «Reloj de agua»: imagen que es a la vez concepto, emoción instantánea, percepción visual y proceso:

> En la gota de agua
> parpadea
> la aguja inmutable
> del tiempo
> y del no tiempo.
>
> Como el hueso en la carne
> el sol está dentro de la gota suspensa.
>
> Interior insolación del tiempo. (54)

Las grandes maravillas de este libro son las *tannkas*. Con ellas, siempre fiel a su búsqueda de esencialidad y purificación, Amusco se acerca a la tradición arábigo-andaluza, de acuerdo con su procedencia sevillana. En la mayor parte de estos brevísimos poemas el lector puede seguir la transformación, no pocas veces basada en la sinestesia, que está ocurriendo:

> ¿No has visto
> cómo la luna se ha roto
> al pasar entre los pinos?
> ¡Qué blanca viene
> la fragancia del bosque! (61)

> Llueve en el mar.
> La barca asciende,
> leve, suspendida en la lluvia.
> El cielo va llenándose
> de balanceos. (66)

Como resumen de la obra de Amusco aparecida hasta hoy casi se podría citar el famoso poema de Juan Ramón «Vino, primero, pura». A través de la experimentación con el versículo más amplio, con la palabra desbordante, ha llegado a una esencialidad y pureza casi absolutas, donde vibran ya no los versos, sino la poesía misma.[36]

* * *

Autor de un solo libro de poesía, *El lugar del aire* (Hiperión, 1981), Luis Suñén, quien se ha destacado como crítico de la narrativa, ha empezado a escribir poesía ya mucho antes. Su dedicación a la novela le coloca en una situación particular: puede acercarse a la poesía con doble perspectiva, con una distancia que no siempre consiguen los autores inmersos en un solo género. Probablemente ha ganado con esperar — como Jorge Guillén — con la publicación de su libro: en él se presenta de pronto con una voz más depurada y más personal que la que se percibía en sus publicaciones esporádicas en revistas. Su poética indica cierta afinidad con Guillén, aunque no le mencione entre sus autores preferidos: «la necesidad de fundirse a la vida por la palabra, de participar en la existencia desde ella, de utilizarla como modo de desvelar el presente. ... Me parece cada vez más importante la necesidad de construir una poesía que jamás abdique de su consistencia formal. El logro de la belleza a través de la palabra no implica claudicar en el compromiso de lo escrito ni restringe la capacidad de comunicación».[37] Las semejanzas con Guillén se dan tanto en la actitud afirmativa como en la forma cuidada, en el verso reducido a las esencias.

Los poemas de *El lugar del aire* son todos breves, nominales. Frecuentemente, el verso final representa el punto de llegada, el fin del proceso: «El ser ya crece en su distancia» (14). No pocas veces aparece el adverbio *ya* usado con significado semejante al que se encuentra en la poesía de Guillén: para señalar la alegría del resultado esperado. Incluso los títulos de sus poemas hacen pensar en *Cántico*: «Situación exacta de la luz», «Suma», «Vida en equilibrio», «Región luciente» que habla de «la memoria del aire», y el último, «Figura», donde «El espacio alcanza su definición exacta» (61). Predominan el presente o el infinitivo, pero el verbo no abunda. Las cosas son, y esto basta: «La vida reconoce su materia: / su cauce es el instante» (18). Se subraya la importancia de la mirada. Como en los poemas de M.V. Atencia, no hay narración, sólo constatación, frecuentemente por yuxtaposición. La tensión, el dinamismo son interiores: en estos poemas se percibe un movimiento casi esculpido, comparable al de «Estatua ecuestre» de Guillén. Como Guillén, usa con gran maestría el encabalgamiento y la rima interior, y la luz y la música son referentes constantes. Sugiere que «la emoción es la forma» (31) y hace mención de «clara pasión de lo concreto» (32). Su énfasis en la vida, en el esfuerzo, es casi orteguiano.

Se ha hablado a veces de la poesía de Jorge Guillén como intelectual. Siles utiliza este término al tratar de definir la de Suñén, matizando exactamente: «[Se] sitúa .. entre los creadores de más precisa y contenida enunciación. Y ello, no por carencia de medios expresivos – que en su caso no la hay ... – sino por una rigurosa voluntad de contención y de decantamiento, que hacen de su escritura un novedoso y firme *razonar*. Pero un razonar *distinto*, que arranca, no de lo real-sensible, sino de lo sensual intelectualizado, y que convierte el *logos* en reflejo de sí y en *reflexión*». Definición que recuerda la que ofrecía Salinas al referirse a la poesía de Guillén, llamándola una ordenación poética del entusiasmo. Siles señala que la de Suñén no es «meta-física, sino *fisicidad* como elemento constitutivo e integrante de la condición *aceptada* (y en Suñén, *aceptable*) de la Vida», lo cual hace recordar al Guillén de *Final*: «¿Metafísica? – Física» (78). Subraya su vitalismo, su fe de vida y hace notar que se trata «de una vida, fenomenológicamente contemplada, que es Guillén y Ortega».[38]

Tal vez la voz clara de Suñén resulte menos contagiosa e invasiva que la de Guillén, pero se trata aún de su primer libro. Su obra parece ser hoy una de las más afirmativas, como demuestra su poema «Límite», cuyo título probablemente haya que entender en términos de Wittgenstein, como la forma del mundo:

> Voluntad de vida,
> plenitud cierta.
> Arco de luz
> o árbol amarillo.
> Velo de la sombra
> que fue. Círculo,
> La alegría todo canto
> consuma, Nunca
> el gozo sin este cielo.
> Todo es y a todo vuelvo. (23)

* * *

La poesía de Jaime Siles presenta el caso más interesante en nuestro contexto. Su relación con Guillén casi se podría estudiar como una lucha (en términos de Harold Bloom). Esto parece evidente en una de sus últimas entregas, «Mecánica celeste»,[39] que es una *reprise* obvia de «Mecánica celeste» de Guillén (desarrollo en tres partes, elementos e incluso léxico comunes, condensación), pero no exactamente en el modo de los «homenajes» que ofrecía Guillén. Se crea conscientemente un poema *nuevo*. El marco de esta exposición no permite proceder a un análisis más detallado de los dos poemas, que sería fascinante.

Siles es, entre los jóvenes poetas, el autor que muestra la evolución más impresionante. Experto en teoría literaria y cada vez más interesado en filosofía, está forjando un lenguaje escueto lleno de carga explosiva. Sus escritos críticos echan luz tanto sobre su propia poética como sobre su poesía. Particularmente interesantes para las reflexiones presentes son su libro sobre la poesía barroca y su ensayo sobre la poesía de Guillén. En varios trabajos suyos se nota casi una obsesión por la fenomenología estructural: es lo que intenta hacer con su propia poesía. En Jorge Guillén admira la capacidad de crear una poesía ácrona, pero a la vez histórica, y de componer con la imagen profunda (ideia), a la que reduce la realidad, así como la sabia unión de inteligencia y pasión que producen condensación y concentración casi absolutas.

Resulta interesante comparar lo que dice Siles en su poética sobre la realidad con la actitud de Guillén frente a ella. Siles habla de devolver la realidad a la Realidad como la tarea principal del poeta. Para Guillén esta tarea consiste en manifestar su asombro frente a la realidad y cantarla. Siles insiste en la necesidad de transformar los nombres hasta el sustrato primigenio. Guillén extrae estos sustratos de las cosas y luego las nombra. La condensación de las esencias en *Cántico* lleva a la afirmación y al canto jubiloso. El último Siles pone cada vez más énfasis en el eco y el silencio. José Olivio Jiménez ha visto con acierto su lucha por la palabra esencial, por el poder fundador de la imagen y se ha referido a su quehacer poético como «ejercicio de tensión y salvación».[40] Lo que no es fácil descubrir en Siles es el gozo guilleniano: en el trasfondo yace la amenaza de la nada.

El silencio se asoma alguna vez también en Guillén, pero con un matiz muy distinto. Sirvan como ejemplo unos versos de «Repertorio de junio» (*Homenaje*):

No te comparo a la flor,
Eres sin nombre tú misma,
¡Oh capital de mi culto!
Mi destino en ti se abisma.
Sea el silencio en tu honor.
(*Aire nuestro*, 1363)

Aquí asoma lo que Ramón Xirau — señalado por Siles como la fuente principal de las reflexiones sobre el silencio entre los jóvenes — llamaría «teología de lo indecible».[41] Es un silencio positivo, casi místico, y en parte temático. El silencio que surge en las páginas de los últimos libros de Siles parece ser debido a una necesidad de negar y de veras se encamina hacia el enmudecer. También en otros aspectos se puede descubrir un matiz diferenciador. La «mirada posesiva de estirpe guilleniana» que destaca Rodríguez Padrón en la obra de Siles logra abstraer de la realidad las estructuras profundas, pero el impulso esencial es diferente, y el resultado surge como una realidad creada, densa, vibrante, pero sin la nota de júbilo tan característica en Guillén.[42]

La actitud que más frecuentemente se trasluce en Siles es el escepticismo; su cosmovisión se acerca probablemente más a la de Aleixandre. Pero de Guillén le vienen el énfasis en la figura, el arte de contrapunto, el interés por la música no sólo del verso, sino del universo. Las diferencias son siempre de matiz; por ejemplo, aun en la búsqueda de las esencias está presente en sus versos la cultura: se trata de una abstracción de segundo grado. En realidad, no hay que sorprenderse por el culturalismo presente en sus poemas, sino más bien por la depuración conseguida, si se considera que en su primer libro, *Génesis de la luz* (1969) aún aparecían imágenes como «taxis azules que mueren en agosto» (*Poesía* 17). Entre los primeros poemas y sus últimas composiciones el único denominador común parece ser la muerte. Incluso dentro del delgado *Cánon*, su libro-clave (1973), la evolución es constante. Es allí donde ofrece ya una condensación impresionante. Se pueden percibir en él algunas notas reminiscentes de Guillén, aunque siempre queda la diferencia de matiz:

> Devuélveme, memoria poderosa,
> la conciencia profunda del instante.
> Tocar la cantidad de esencia doble
> y no dejar jamás de ser materia.
>
> La posesión de límite que encierro
> hacia un espacio sin final me lanza,
> que es perfección, dominio, maravilla:
> totalidad de ser únicamente. (42)

Se ha aludido ya a cómo, buscando lo mismo, los dos poetas desembocan en caminos y procedimientos divergentes. *Cántico* representa afirmación y crecimiento; *Poesía*, reducción y negación. Se concibe la poesía como lenguaje construido. Por consiguiente, se puede referir a ella como materia, que es, sin embargo, inseparable del concepto, no sencillamente «maravillas concretas». La forma se da como elaboración consciente y como tema. Se subraya la importancia de la figura a través de la disposición tipográfica, círculos, distribución geométrica del poema, juegos de inversión simétrica, pero casi nunca se llega a una simetría total, como si se quisiera insinuar la imposibilidad de perfección absoluta. En los últimos libros se encuentra la palabra esencial, pero a la vez este lenguaje se vuelve casi críptico; de la lógica se deriva hacia el silencio:

Equilibrio de luz
en el sosiego.
Mínima tromba.
Ensoñación. Quietud.
Todo:
un espacio sin voz
hacia lo hondo oculto. (*Poesía* 28)

La luz misma es diferente, no incita a júbilo:

> Sobre la luz delgada sólo puntos.
> En el centro del iris sólo gotas,
> que la noche revierte
> —punto o gota—
> en el delgado centro
> de la luz. (*Poesía* 129)

En el último libro, *Música de agua* (1983), menudean juegos conceptistas:

Un espejo vacío y un abanico blanco
    la grafía ya es
abanico vacío en el espejo en blanco
    que cada cosa es.
    («Disoluciones» 49)

Totalidad de ti
desde este todo
que vacío vacío
en el vacío
de un único jardín espejeante.
    («Idioma» 55)

En este libro se puede observar una progresión hacia la noche, hacia el vacío, una insistencia cada vez más fuerte en lo negro, es decir, *sin* color, relacionado con la disolución y la nada: «tinta extinta»; «La tierra de la noche: alfabeto nocturno de la nada». En su resumen panorámico de la poesía de hoy, refiriéndose a los poetas-profesores, decía García Martín que «la universidad devora a sus mejores hijos» (*Las Voces y los Ecos* 53). A su vez, Amparo Amorós señala que gracias a *Canon* de Siles se abre «una salida al 'cul de sac' de la estética de los novísimos» (20). La esencialidad y depuración que se logran en *Música de agua* son impresionantes. Pero al llegar al último poema, «Final», se vuelve completamente imposible predecir qué rumbo seguirá esta poesía en los años por venir:

> Ningún sonido o signo se te impone.
> Nada de lo que eres
> te invita a ser su voz.
> En vano insiste.
>   Sólo
> este silencio firme te acompaña.
> Este silencio
> más tuyo ahora
> que tu propia voz.

El invisible punto
ya ha llegado.
Ya sólo en ti
final
la transparencia. (74)

Resumiendo lo expuesto a lo largo de estas consideraciones, y
sin olvidar su propósito de homenaje, se podría repetir, al pregun-
tarse qué eco ha tenido la poesía de Jorge Guillén entre los poetas
más jóvenes, lo que Siles ha formulado acerca de la relación de
Góngora con los poetas del 27: «Cada uno realizará, en su paráfrasis
de Góngora, la realización de sí».[43] La presencia de Guillén no es
tan imperiosa ni alcanza a todos, pero su actitud y su poema logrado
permanecen como ejemplo y modelo para algunos: una actitud que
desparrama luz, una luz interior bellamente sintetizada por Angel
González en su «Glosas en homenaje a Jorge Guillén»:

Vistas así las cosas,
iluminadas por amor tan claro
¿cómo van a negarse?

Dóciles, entregadas
a su más alto vuelo,
se demoran, esperan, se eternizan.
....
Rasga el aire el silencio y ...
¡Luz ilesa!
He ahí la eternidad, en dos palabras.[44]

NOTAS

[1] Jorge Guillén prefería la denominación «grupo». Jaime Gil de Biedma
declara en una de sus recientes entrevistas: «Las promociones literarias son, en
principio, operaciones de autopromoción, de lanzamiento literario, es decir, de
política literaria. ... Luego, los catedráticos se lo toman en serio y se dedican a
buscar puntos de afinidad entre los que las componen. Pero eso ya es una
operación hecha a posteriori y, por supuesto, una falsificación de la realidad»
(Jesús Fernández Palacios, «Con Jaime Gil de Biedma, colgados de la poesía».
Fin de Siglo 5 [1983] 70). Según José Luis García Martín, la última promoción
habría surgido en 1976: Emilio Barón, Julio Llamazares, Felipe Núñez, José
Gutiérrez («Introducción», *Las Voces y los Ecos* [Madrid: Júcar, 1980]).

[2] En el estudio preliminar de Fanny Rubio y José Luis Falcó a *Poesía
española contemporánea (1939-1980)* se subraya «el sentimiento de inuti-
lidad de la literatura, de la poesía, la pérdida de la fe en el valor activo de la
palabra poética» entre los novísimos (Madrid: Alhambra, 1981, 76). Lo corrobo-
ran declaraciones como la de Lázaro Santana en su «Como una poética, pero
no»: «Pienso que un poema no debiera estar, sino ser (un pequeño tiempo)
porque / un poema es algo perfectamente inútil» (*Poetas españoles poscon-*

temporáneos, ed. J. Batlló [Barcelona: El Bardo, 1974] 61), o la repetida insistencia en «la podredumbre», también de la palabra, en *Dialéctica de las sombras* de Manuel Ruiz Amescua (Barcelona: Anthropos, 1979).

[3]«Sin nombre», *Retratos con nombre, Obras completas* (Madrid: Aguilar, 1968) 1040. La negación es más fuerte aún en «El poeta se acuerda de su vida», *Poemas de la consumación* (Barcelona: Plaza & Janés, 1968): «Las palabras mueren. / Bellas son al sonar, mas nunca duran» (82).

[4]«Para un esteta», *Quinta del 42, Poesías completas* (Madrid: Giner, 1967) 294.

[5]«Posturas del poeta ante su palabra: la época de posguerra», en este volumen.

[6]«Intertextuality in Selected Spanish Poets since 1939: Intertext/ Poetics/Reader», en este volumen.

[7]María Victoria Atencia, «Sazón», *Cuatro sonetos, Ex Libris* (Madrid: Visor, 1984) 149.

[8]Piénsese en las ya citadas *Poesía española contemporánea* de Rubio y Falcó y *Las Voces y los Ecos* de García Martín, o su más reciente *Poesía española 1982-1983* (Madrid: Hiperión, 1983); Concepción G. Moral y Rosa María Pereda, *Joven poesía española* (Madrid: Cátedra, 1979); Elena de Jongh Rossel, *Florilegium* (Madrid: Espasa-Calpe, 1982); Víctor Pozanco, *Nueve poetas del resurgimiento* (Barcelona: Ambito, 1976); o G.L. Solner, *Poesía Española Hoy* (Madrid: Visor, 1982), que apenas incluye poetas verdaderamente jóvenes.

[9]Carlos Bousoño ofrece una explicación persuasiva acerca de su popularidad en «La poesía de Guillermo Carnero», estudio preliminar a Guillermo Carnero, *Ensayo de una teoría de la visión* (Barcelona: I. Peralta, 1979) 25.

[10]«Los novísimos, o la poesía de la década prodigiosa», *Los Cuadernos del Norte* 5 (1981): 60.

[11]«Centro» 9.

[12]Este es un silencio muy diferente al que Florence Yudin ha analizado en la obra de Jorge Guillén: *The Vibrant Silence in Jorge Guillén* (Chapel Hill: North Carolina University Press, 1974).

[13]«Yo soy», *Y otros poemas* (Buenos Aires: Muchnik, 1973) 321.

[14]«La generación del lenguaje», *Poesía* 5-6 (1979-1980): 246.

[15]Si descontamos los primeros intentos en publicaciones periodísticas, hoy reunidos en *Hacia «Cántico».*, *Escritos de los años 20*, ed. K.M. Sibbald (Barcelona: Ariel, 1980).

[16]Amparo Amorós Moltó, «La retórica del silencio», *Los Cuadernos del Norte* 16 (1982): 18-27, donde refiere a otro trabajo de José-Miguel Ullán sobre «la plaga del silencio».

[17]*Lecturas de Octavio Paz* (Barcelona: Anagrama, 1980) 10.

[18]«La expresión», *Final* (Barcelona: Barral, 1981) 58.

[19]«Three Moments of Post-Civil War Poetry», en este volumen.

[20]*Poetas españoles poscontemporáneos* 155.

[21]Entrevista citada 68. Son interesantes sus consideraciones acerca de las correcciones, que confirman el énfasis en la fuerte ligazón del poema con el momento vivido, no búsqueda de continuidad e integración en un conjunto total.

[22]*El barroco en la poesía española. Conscienciación lingüística y tensión histórica* (Madrid: Doncel, 1975) 93.

[23]«Poesía en la década de los 70: En torno a los 'Novísimos'», *Insula* 410 (1981): 4.

[24]*Vicente Aleixandre ou une poésie du suspens. Recherches sur le réel et l'imaginaire* (Perpignan: Editions du Castellet, 1980).

[25]«Materia única», *En un vasto dominio, op. cit.* 963. Verso que Antonio Carvajal pone como epígrafe a su *Naturaleza ofrecida* (*Tigres en el jardín, Extravagante jerarquía* [Madrid: Hiperión, 1983] 22).

[26]«Ante una nueva promoción poética», *La Nueva Estafeta* 7 (1979): 92-93.

[27]*Poesía (1969-1980)* (Madrid: Visor, 1982) 7.

[28]En *Una promoción desheredada: La poética del 50*, ed. Antonio Hernández (Bilbao: Zero, 1978) 325.

[29]*El País* (semanal), 13 febrero 1984.

[30]Cito por la edición de *Diversificaciones* (Valencia: Fernando Torres, 1982) 55 y 56.

[31]*Extravagante jerarquía* 28.

[32]«Dos versos de Claudio Rodríguez y una prosa de Pedro Salinas: Ensayo de reconstrucción», *Insula* 444-445 (1983): 7.

[33]«Caprichos», *Hora de poesía* 30 (1983): 46.

[34]«María Victoria Atencia o el triunfo de la belleza», *Los Cuadernos del Norte* 16 (1982): 38. Clto siempre por *El mundo de M.V.* (Madrid: Insula, 1978) y *El coleccionista* (Sevilla: Gráficas del Sur, 1979).

[35]*Poesía* 17 (1983): 30. Los libros de Amusco: *Esencias de los días* (Madrid: Insula, 1976); *El sol en Sagitario* (Barcelona: Ambito literario, 1978); *Del agua, del fuego y otras purificaciones* (Barcelona: Los libros de la Frontera, 1983).

[36]Sería curioso investigar un fenómeno que tal vez no sea más que una coincidencia: en los poemas depurados de más de un autor se acentúa la presencia del agua: Amusco; *Música de agua* de Jaime Siles; «Juegos del agua» de Salvador López Becerra.

[37]*Nueve poetas del resurgimiento* 78. Allí mismo señala «la necesidad de romper a cada momento con la propia obra ya hecha, a través de una autocrítica continua».

[38]«La poesía de Luis Suñén», *Insula* 421 (1981): 12.

[39]*Andalán* 283 (1983): 25-27.

[40]«La palabra existencial y tensa de Jaime Siles», *Diálogos* 12.2 (1976): 33.

[41]Vid. Ramón Xirau, «Maimónides, teólogo de lo indecible», *Palabra y silencio* (México: Siglo XXI, 1968).

[42]Jorge Ridríguez Padrón, «La poesía de Jaime Siles: Notas de aproximación», *Insula* 433 (1982): 3.

[43]«Jorge Guillén: simetría y sistema», *Diversificaciones* 57.

[44]Angel González, *Prosemas o menos* (Santander, 1983) 61-62.